TO TELL THE TRUTH

TO TELL THE TRUTH

Keys to unlocking John's Gospel

by

Clifford W. Kew

UNITED KINGDOM TERRITORY
101 Queen Victoria Street, London EC4P 4EP

Major Clifford W. Kew, MA,
became an a Salvation Army officer in 1957. After
serving as a corps officer in the United Kingdom he
was appointed to the teaching staff of Mazoe
Secondary School, Rhodesia, in 1968, becoming
vice-principal in 1971. Subsequently he served in
the Literary Department, International Headquarters,
both as writer of *The Soldier's Armoury* and editor of
The Officer magazine and at the officers' training
college of the UK Territory. He retired in June 1996.

Typeset by THQ Print and Design Unit
Printed by Hillman Printers (Frome) Ltd
Cover design by Gill Cox

Contents

INTRODUCTION

THERE are many ways in which the study of Scripture may be approached: devotional meditation, the homiletic study of important texts, the scholarly analysis of the text in the original language, and so on.

One helpful but relatively easy way to study John's Gospel is by looking at various characteristic phrases used by the writer, phrases which crop up repeatedly in the Gospel. These may be regarded as verbal keys, with which we may unlock the Gospel, for they do not appear to be just accidental characteristics of the thought processes of John (or of Jesus) in the sense that people often have unconscious habits of speech and hackneyed phrases which they use a great deal. For example, some people use 'basically' ad nauseum, or 'sort of', or 'you know'. John's verbal keys seem much more deliberate than this. They seem to be carefully placed and to fit into the structure of the Gospel, part of the skeleton around which the sinews and skin of his body of truth about Jesus are built up. Examples of such phrases are 'the Word', 'I am', 'sign', 'I am telling you the truth'. By a deliberate analysis of such verbal signposts we may, almost incidentally, come to a deep understanding both of the historical detail and the spiritual truth of the gospel.

There is still much discussion about the author and date of this Bible book. The traditional view was that it was written by the fisherman John who was one of the twelve disciples—brother of James and son of Zebedee. The fact that it is carefully constructed and gives evidence of familiarity with the characteristics of Greek philosophy was accounted for by assuming that John had by the date of writing acquired a good deal of scholarship and was an elder statesman at the church of Ephesus. This would give a late date to the writing—perhaps as late as 90 AD. It was also assumed that John's Gospel was written with a knowledge of the other three 'synoptic' Gospels ('synoptic' means 'sharing the same viewpoint'), but had a rather different purpose from them.

Others have concluded that the writer was a different John, perhaps a follower of John the disciple, or even that the Johannine literature (the Gospel, the three letters of John, and Revelation) was the product of a community living in the spirit of John. This might give an even later, second century, date.

In more recent times, opinion has swung to an acceptance of an early date, and to a view that the Gospel is just as historically reliable as the Synoptics, though it uses some different sources of material, and emphasises different aspects of the ministry of Jesus. For example, John emphasises the time spent in Judea and Jerusalem rather than in Galilee. He stresses the time before the arrest of John the Baptist whereas the Synoptics give less notice to that. And the overall time-scale he uses is an apparent three-year public ministry rather than the one-year ministry suggested by the other Gospel writers. One writer has even suggested a date of writing between 40 and 65 AD, which could make John's Gospel the earliest of the four.

Whoever the writer was, and whenever he wrote, there is no doubt about the Gospel being an authentic record and a most valuable interpretation of the life of our Lord. If we look at the verbal patterns already referred to, an understanding of the purpose and method of the writer will emerge, whoever he was. This method of studying the Gospel has the advantage for the ordinary reader of not requiring any great background of scholarship, but only an eye for verbal links and patterns. In this way much that is profitable for meditation may be obtained.

Note: Scripture quotations are from the *Good News Bible* unless otherwise indicated.

KEY 1

THE NAMES OF THE SON OF GOD
('The Word' and 'I am')

WE know that the John who wrote the book of Revelation was exiled on the isle of Patmos, fairly near to the city of Ephesus which was on what is now the Turkish mainland. Ephesus was the most important city in Asia Minor and there was a strong tradition in the Early Church that the John who wrote the Gospel lived there to an old age. It does seem that the Greek language and culture which held sway in such places as Ephesus did have quite an influence on the writer of John's Gospel. This fact and the assumption that this Gospel was of a late date caused many to assume that it was a kind of late Greek revision of the story of Jesus and was thus less original and less historically reliable than the other three Gospels. One scholar concluded that John's Gospel does not belong to 'the historical books of primitive Christianity but to its [later] Hellenistic [Greek] doctrinal writings'.

'The word'

But the 'Greekness' of the book can be exaggerated. It is primarily highlighted by the fact that the prologue or introduction (1:1-18) is composed in the style of Greek philosophers—somewhat abstract and academic—and uses a phrase that is typical of Greek philosophy. It refers to 'the *logos*'—the literal translation of which is 'word'—which in this context means the expression or demonstration of what God is. This term is taken as an introduction and explanation of the story of Jesus, Son of God.

However, the rest of the Gospel does not continue in this style and does not use *logos* (word), or the prologue's other key words of *charis* (grace), and *pleroma* (fullness). It has therefore been suggested that this prologue may have been added later to the basic text by a group of followers of John who lived in a Hellenistic situation such as Ephesus. Whether we accept this or not, it is a mistake to base our understanding of the whole Gospel on the style and content of its introduction.

1

The fact which has often been lost sight of is that, if the prologue has a strong Greek influence, then the body of John's Gospel has an even stronger dependence on *Jewish* ideas of God. One key to understanding this is the use of the phrase 'I am'. This was of course God's name as he gave it to Moses: 'I am who I am. This is what you must say to them: "The one who is called I AM has sent me to you"' (Exodus 3:14). The *Authorised Version* reads: 'I am that I am' and the use of 'I am he' elsewhere in the Old Testament is similar (see Deuteronomy 32:39; Isaiah 43:10 and 46:4 in the *AV*). We may find this Hebrew name for God to be enigmatic and unsatisfactory but we may paraphrase it as: 'I am the One who is' or 'I am the God who always exists' or, as one writer has it, 'You can depend on me!'

'I am'

When we come to the New Testament, we find the equivalent Greek phrase to be *'ego eimi'*, which is an emphatic form of 'I' and is perhaps most clearly translated by 'I myself am'. So when Jesus uses the phrase 'I am' it has special and unmistakable reference to God. There is no doubt that one of the intentional emphases of John's Gospel is on the divinity of Christ. So when, as John records it, Jesus uses the phrase 'I am', he is claiming to be God, a higher claim than is obvious in the other Gospels. 'You will die in your sins if you do not believe that "I Am Who I Am". . . . When you lift up the Son of Man, you will know that "I Am Who I Am"; then you will know that I do nothing on my own authority, but I say only what the Father has instructed me to say. . . .' (8:24, 28). Jesus claims to have existed before Abraham: 'Before Abraham was born, "I Am"' (8:58); he is the timeless Son of God. His claim is 'The Father and I are one' (10:30). This is just as firmly an expression of his eternal status in Jewish terms, as is the use of *logos* in Greek terms.

And it is this Gospel which records Jesus using the same phrase in the seven great affirmations, the famous seven sayings which begin with 'I am' (*ego eimi*), sentences which use various symbols to express the nature of his ministry:

6:35	I am the bread of life;
8:12	I am the light of the world;
10:7, 9	I am the gate for the sheep;
10:11	I am the good shepherd;
11:25	I am the resurrection and the life;
14:6	I am the way, the truth, and the life;
15:1	I am the real vine.

It seems that John consciously tries to avoid using the phrase 'I am' in any more mundane way. It has been said that 'there is in this Gospel no "ego" except the "Ego" ("I am") of Jesus the Son of God'. John himself does not intrude into his narrative, except for a curious, shy, little 'I suppose' in 21:25. Otherwise, he seems to go out of his way to avoid the limelight and is alluded to only by the somewhat anonymous phrases: 'the disciple whom Jesus loved' or 'that other disciple' (see John 21:20; also 13:23-25; 18:15, 16; 19:26, 27; 20:1-10; 21:7). He deliberately leaves the stage clear for a solo performance of the great 'I am'.

So the Gospel which begins with a prologue couched in language that would be familiar to Greek readers, with its use of the word *logos*, has at its heart this repeated phrase *ego eimi* ('I myself am') which was especially familiar and significant to Jewish readers. Thus it is not just the Gospel rewritten to make it acceptable to Gentile readers. It is based soundly on Jewish theology and on the teaching of Christ about himself.

KEY 2

THE TIME, THE PLACE

WE have seen that one fairly common but somewhat mistaken idea regarding the fourth Gospel is that it is a late Greek version of the gospel story. Another misleading emphasis is that it is a 'spiritual' Gospel rather than a historical one like the other three Gospels, that it is a series of teaching passages or sermons associated with certain happenings rather than a straightforward biographical account of the ministry of Jesus. An Early Church scholar, Clement of Alexandria, seems to have originated this misunderstanding. He lived in the second half of the second century AD, and tried to account for the differences between John's Gospel and the other three by saying: 'Last of all, John, aware that the physical [or historical] facts had been clearly set forth in the other Gospels . . . composed a *spiritual* Gospel.' This assumes that it was the last of the Gospels to be written and had a different purpose from the others.

Ever since, some people have tended to misinterpret Clement's comment as meaning that the writer John was not concerned with historical fact so much as spiritual truth. That interpretation cannot be sustained if one reads his Gospel with an open mind. It is true that John does bring out the *meaning* of Jesus' deeds and words, but he does also give a lot of exact detail. After the prologue (1:1-18), which admittedly has rather an abstract feel about it, John goes straight into a day-by-day diary of one week when Jesus first 'went public', and the Gospel draws to its conclusion with a long and almost hour-by-hour account of the last week he was physically present with his disciples, from Palm Sunday to Easter Sunday. In between there are many specific details to which the teaching is anchored. He is, in fact, remarkably specific about times, numbers and other details.

A day-by-day diary

If we look at the sections following the prologue we will see the structure of the day-by-day diary quite clearly:

4

The Event		The Time	The Place
1:19-28	John baptising	Day 1	Bethany beyond Jordan
1:29-34	John witnesses to Jesus	Day 2	Bethany beyond Jordan
1:35-42	Two disciples follow Jesus	Day 3	Bethany beyond Jordan
1:43-51	Philip and Nathanael	Day 4	Galilee
2:1-11	The wedding miracle	Day 6	Cana in Galilee
2:12	Family holiday	Few Days	Capernaum
2:13-25	Cleansing the Temple	Passover	Jerusalem
3:1-21	Conversation with Nicodemus	Night	Jerusalem
3:22-36	Baptising in Jordan	After Passover	Aenon near Salim

Thus in the first two or three chapters John several times makes remarks about the lapse of time between one event and another: 'the next day' (1:29, 35, 43); 'two days later' (2:1); 'a few days' (2:12).

Detailed facts

Throughout the Gospel, John is very exact about the time when events took place:

> Jesus invites the disciples to his lodgings at *4 pm* (1:39).
> Nicodemus meets Jesus *'one night'* (3:2).
> Jesus talks to the woman at the well *'about noon'* (4:6).
> The fever left the government official's son at *'one o'clock yesterday afternoon'* (4:52).
> The disciples crossed the lake *'when evening came'* (6:16).
> Jesus is moved to the governor's palace *'early in the morning'* (18:28).
> When Pilate takes Jesus out to the crowd it is *'almost noon'* (19:14).
> Jesus appears to the disciples *'late that Sunday evening'* (20:19).
> He stands at the water's edge *'as the sun was rising'* (21:4).

There is nothing vague or 'spiritual' about these details. They are the marks of an account of historical fact and, most probably, of personal experience.

John is also very specific about numbers:

> *Six water jars* each containing about *a hundred litres* were used at Cana (2:6).
> The woman at the well had had *five husbands* (4:18).
> The man healed at Bethzatha (also translated Bethesda or Bethsaida) had been ill for *38 years* (5:5).

5

> Five loaves of barley bread and two fishes were used to feed about 5,000 men (6:9).
>
> The disciples rowed 'about five or six kilometres' (6:19).
>
> Judas wanted the ointment to be sold for 'three hundred silver coins' (12:5).
>
> Jesus' clothes were divided into four parts (19:23).
>
> Joseph brought 'about thirty kilogrammes of spices' to bury Jesus (19:39).
>
> The disciples were 'about a hundred metres' from land (21:8) when they caught 153 fishes (21:11).

John is exact also about places: Bethany east of the Jordan (1:28), distinguishing it from the Bethany near Jerusalem (11:18); Cana in Galilee (2:1); Capernaum (2:12); Aenon near Salim (3:23); Jacob's well at Sychar (4:5, 6); and so on. He is specific about places in Jerusalem too, eg, the pool of Bethzatha (5:2); the pool of Siloam (9:7-11); Golgotha (19:17), etc.

There are in John's Gospel, also, a number of narrative incidents which are not in the other Gospels. These concern Nicodemus (3:1-21); the Samaritan woman (4:1-42); the paralysed man at the pool (5:1-18); the man born blind (chapter 9); Lazarus and his sisters, Martha and Mary (11:1-53); and the footwashing at the last supper (13:1-11). In this Gospel also certain characters emerge much more clearly, eg, Andrew (1:40-42; 6:8; 12:22); and Thomas (11:16; 20:24-29).

Characterisation

So John includes all sorts of vivid detail and lively characterisation which would have little point if he were merely seeking to propound *spiritual* truth. It is inconceivable that he invented all these details. It all suggests an eyewitness account different from, but no less reliable than, those in the Synoptics. He may in fact have gone out of his way to include details that the others had left out.

If John's Gospel is 'spiritual', therefore, that does not mean that it is unhistorical. He very often refers to 'the time . . . the place' when and where events happened, and if we note these references to the circumstances in which they happened, we shall find that we are turning another key in the unlocking process of this wonderful Gospel.

KEY 3

THE SEVEN SIGNS

THE third key on our bunch which gives access to the truths of John's Gospel is the realisation that the book has a deliberate structure and that its structure is closely related to seven 'signs', as the *Revised Version* correctly translates the Greek word '*semeion*', which means 'a visible indication of secret power or truth'. Unfortunately the *Good News Bible* somewhat obscures this by using the word 'miracle'. Perhaps the *New International Version* is preferable in translating the word by 'miraculous sign'. John selects seven happenings as special signs of God's power. They point up the stark power of Jesus as the Son of God.

The signs are:

2:1-11	the turning of water into wine at the marriage at Cana;
4:46-54	the healing of the son of a government official;
5:1-9	the healing at the pool of Bethzatha;
6:1-15	the feeding of the 5000;
6:16-21	Jesus walking on the water;
9:1-41	the healing of a man who had been born blind;
11:1-53	the raising of Lazarus from death.

Miraculous signs

The Gospel writer is sometimes quite specific in highlighting these 'miraculous signs'. For example: 'This was the beginning of the signs of Jesus' (2:11, literal translation); 'This was the second miraculous sign that Jesus performed, having come from Judea to Galilee' (4:54, *NIV*); 'After the people saw the miraculous sign that Jesus did . . .' (6:14, *NIV*).

No doubt there were other effective signs or miracles (see, for example, 2:23, *NIV*: 'Many people saw the miraculous signs he was doing and believed . . .'; and 11:47, *NIV*: 'Here is this man performing many miraculous signs.') But John selects these seven as specially meaningful and ties his accounts of the teaching of Jesus to them.

7

(Incidentally, at least one scholar does not count the walking on the water but makes up the blessed number seven by including the catching of 153 fish in 21:1-13, though this chapter may be a late addition to the Gospel.)

On the other hand, there are recorded occasions when Jesus refused to perform a miraculous sign to order. One was when the Jews asked him to justify the cleansing of the Temple with a sign that would authenticate his right to carry out such an action. 'What miraculous sign can you show us to prove your authority to do all this?' (2:18, *NIV*). They were ready only to challenge his position rather than to accept his power. However, he did offer them a sign that they dared not accept. He asked them to destroy the Temple and he would rebuild it in three days (2:19-22). But, if we are to take this passage literally, they dared not risk their beloved Temple, and so failed to see the evidence of the power of the one whose dwelling-place it was.

Looking for a sign

We should ask ourselves whether we are ready to see the signs staring us in the face, which authenticate the claims of Jesus on our lives. Are we always looking for a sign which will meet our criteria, a sign which will allow us to cling to the traditional accoutrements of religious life, while we fail to be aware of the spiritual presence of him who is the source and completion of our religion?

Another such occasion when Jesus refused to give a sign was when he refused a repeat performance of the feeding of the 5,000 on the day after the original miracle (6:25-33).

As we have seen, chapter 21 may be a late addition to the Gospel, brought in with the specific aim of re-establishing the position of Peter as a leader of the band of apostles. This would mean that John 20:30, 31 would contain the last sentence of the original Gospel. It is clear from these verses that John had a specific aim and method in his selection of signs—to demonstrate the power of the Son of God by means of miracles—but that these seven were only a selection: 'These have been written in order that you may believe that Jesus is the Messiah, the Son of God, and that through your faith in him you may have life.' As S. S. Smalley writes:

> The seven signs . . . together . . . have a vital part to play in the plan of the whole gospel. Not only do they provide it with a unifying framework; they also supply it with a centre by illustrating repeatedly its leading theme: life in Christ.

KEY 4

THE DISCOURSES

BEFORE we leave the consideration of the signs, we should note that many, if not all of them, are associated with a passage of teaching in the form of a discourse. The healing of the invalid at Bethzatha on the Sabbath gives rise to a discourse about the authority of Jesus (5:19-47). The feeding of the 5,000 is followed by teaching about Jesus as the bread of life (6:25-69). The healing of the blind man is followed by a passage about spiritual blindness (9:35-41). The raising of Lazarus occasions teaching on eternal life incorporating the 'I am' saying, 'I am the resurrection and the life' (11:17-44). Identifying these and other discourses is another key to the understanding of John's Gospel.

Discursive teaching

We have seen that Clement's comment about John's Gospel being a 'spiritual Gospel' must not push us into the theory that it is unreliable or vague on matters of time, place, and so on. He is clearly talking about a historical Jesus. Nevertheless, it is quite true that this fourth Gospel does have a very different atmosphere about it from the three Synoptic Gospels. There are many extended passages of teaching, each about one clear theme, in contrast to the type of teaching in the first three Gospels, where short epigrammatic sayings are the rule, and where longer passages generally include a collection of these sayings, rather than a discourse type of teaching.

This difference corresponds to two different kinds of teaching in the ancient world. The Synoptics' epigrammatic style was the one favoured by Jewish teachers. They used short, easily-memorised sentences which the Gospel writers could report word for word, even if they were not always sure of the incident with which they were associated (see, for example, Matthew 7:1-27). It would seem likely, however, that John, who was probably writing in Ephesus to a Greek audience used to the methods of Greek literature and philosophy, may well have adopted their method of *expanding* on the meaning of what the teacher originally said, in the spirit of that teacher (as in John 3:5-13, for example). Perhaps John reports, therefore, what Jesus said 'along with an attempt to bring out the fullness of meaning which years of meditation [and discussion] had found in it' (B. H. Streeter). This is not, however, to falsify the teaching of Jesus, for he himself had said, 'I have much more to tell you, but now it would be too much for you to bear' (16:12), and it was some of those things that the Holy Spirit, the spirit of Jesus, was now revealing to John and possibly his companions.

There are even places where it is not clear in the original Greek where the words of Jesus end and the words of John begin, and different translations put in quotation marks at different places, as there are none in the Greek. (For example, do Jesus' words end at 3:13 or 3:21? The *Good News Bible* ends the quotation marks at 3:13 but the *New International Version* extends the words of Jesus to 3:21.)

Expanded teaching

A number of John's discourses tend to have a similar pattern, which may have been imposed to some extent by the Gospel writer. Debelius points out that 'by foolish questions and very erroneous misunderstandings the hearers repeatedly give Jesus occasion to state again what he has said'. Nicodemus is very slow to understand what Jesus means by being born again, and so gives Jesus opportunity to make his teaching even more clear and plain. The woman of Samaria misunderstands what Jesus says about worship and about the Messiah, until finally Jesus makes it as plain as a pikestaff that he himself who is speaking to her is in fact the Messiah. Likewise, Mary of Bethany fails to understand the possibility of resurrection for her brother Lazarus, and draws out the declaration 'I am the resurrection and the life'. In each case, statement is followed by misunderstanding, producing a fuller statement and expansion of the teaching.

So John has exercised a good deal of craftsmanship in his presentation of Jesus' teaching, probably embracing not just what Jesus said, but also to some extent what Jesus meant, as understood by John and other Church leaders under the inspiration of the Spirit. But this does not mean that he is not working from a historical basis, and we can rightly place our trust in what John writes as gospel truth.

KEY 5

TRUTH TO TELL

PERHAPS the most frequently repeated and most obvious key phrase in John's Gospel is the emphatic formula: 'I am telling you the truth' (*GNB*) or, as the *Authorised Version* puts it, 'Verily, verily, I say unto you'. These are translations of the Greek *'Amen amen lego humin'*. (Note the origin of our word 'Amen' meaning 'verily', 'certainly' or 'truly'.)

The direct highlighting of truth with this phrase is somewhat reminiscent of the Scottish colloquial phrase with which anyone who has lived in or near Glasgow will be familiar: 'A'm tellin' ye!' The special way in which the words are used make them part obvious statement, part argument, part proof, part aggression. Similarly, Jesus makes sure his listeners will pay special attention to his teaching by repeating, 'I am telling you the truth.'

Perhaps we ought to remember that a colloquial phrase in dialect like 'A'm tellin' ye!' is a more likely equivalent of what Jesus actually said than 'Verily, verily, I say unto you'. We hear in the Gospels of the disciples' rough Galilean accent (Matthew 26:73: 'Of course you are one of them. . . . The way you speak gives you away!'), but we may forget that it would have been shared by Jesus himself, and we should not imagine him speaking in the *Authorised Version* English of 1611, or in the equivalent of BBC English or an Oxford accent.

There are in all about 26 'verilies' in John's Gospel and we shall look at them in groups or individually, especially emphasising those from the Holy Week teaching where we have a much more detailed treatment of Jesus' bequest of truth to his disciples than elsewhere.

11

1. THE TRUTH ABOUT OUR SPIRITUALITY
(John 3:1-21)

'I am telling you the truth: no one can see the Kingdom of God unless he is born again' (3:3).

'I am telling you the truth. . . . No one can enter the Kingdom of God unless he is born of water and the Spirit. A person is born physically of human parents, but he is born spiritually of the Spirit' (3:5, 6).

'I am telling you the truth: we speak of what we know and report what we have seen, yet none of you is willing to accept our message' (3:11).

HERE in the third chapter of John's Gospel are the first three statements of Jesus which are highlighted by the key words 'I am telling you the truth'. They emerge from the secret night meeting of Jesus with Nicodemus, a member of the Jewish Sanhedrin or Council, but their inclusion here in John's Gospel makes them the first great open secret of this Gospel—the possibility and necessity of regeneration, of being 'born again', as the basic condition of entering into the Kingdom of God, that state which this book opens wide to us.

The Kingdom of God

'The Kingdom of God' is a phrase used in John rather than 'the Kingdom of Heaven', as in Matthew. The two may be synonymous but certainly 'Kingdom of God' refers to the kingship, sovereignty, authority and rule of God, a state rather than a place. It means allowing God to be king of our lives. That can only happen when the Holy Spirit has brought our spirit to life, when the gale of the Spirit has blown through us and left behind the wind or breath of the spiritual life within us, somewhat as the person who gives the kiss of life breathes strongly into the patient's mouth, so that the patient's own 'breath of life' may once again move in and out of the lungs unaided. The Spirit alone can give us the 'kiss of spiritual life'.

There is an unpredictability about this work of the Spirit: 'The wind blows wherever it wishes; you hear the sound it makes, but you do not know where it comes from or where it is going. It is like that with everyone who is born of the Spirit' (3:8). Dr D. H. C. Read writes:

> These words blow away all our attempts to organise and categorise the experience of the inner life. But you can see the results of the wind—the bending trees, the swirling dust, the soaring kite. You are not asked to define exactly how this inner life has been born in you, or how it grows, but if it is truly there then results will be seen. . . .

Note that nobody is excluded either by their badness or by their goodness from the need to be born again. Again, Dr Read says:

> [Nicodemus] wasn't a profligate, a drunkard or a blasphemer, or even an agnostic, but a most moral, upright citizen, devoted to the faith of his fathers. It is time we stopped thinking of evangelism solely in terms of rescuing the down-and-out and convincing the unbeliever. The gospel is for all. You can't be too religious to be converted by Jesus.

The phrase 'born again' can also be translated 'born from above', but it is obvious that Nicodemus interpreted it as 'born again' because he asks the question 'Can he enter *a second time* into his mother's womb?' (3:4, *Revised Standard Version*). In interpreting the phrase in a physical sense he makes an absurdity of it. As a learned rabbi he should have known better (3:10), but many otherwise-intelligent people still stumble over this obstacle of interpreting literally what is intended figuratively.

Born of water

The reverse is just as dangerous, to take figuratively what is intended literally. Being 'born of water' (3:5) is often taken as a reference to water baptism. That is to take the phrase out of its context, since the previous verse (4) and the following verse (6) both speak of physical birth as distinct from spiritual birth, and it is surely natural to assume that verse 5 is doing the same. Being 'born of water' may well be one valid way of describing physical birth with its breaking of the waters, as Kenneth Taylor observes in a footnote in *The Living Bible*. So in all three verses, it would seem, Jesus is making the distinction between being born physically from the womb and being 'born again' spiritually of the Spirit. The second 'birth' is necessary before we can 'see' or 'enter' the Kingdom of God.

As we have seen previously, there are in John's Gospel at least three places where the person being interviewed by Jesus seems quite obtuse, intentionally or otherwise, and so gives Jesus the opportunity to reiterate his teaching. Nicodemus is a 'teacher in Israel' (3:10) and yet he doesn't seem to have any appreciation of the distinction between the physical and the spiritual. How can he be so 'dim'?

Are we, in spite perhaps of having a religious background or even in spite of taking part in religious activities, so spiritually 'dim' that we do not see the obvious? If so, is this because we do not really want to see the truth in case it requires some change in us that we do not relish? Or have we blinded ourselves to the real truth by deliberately looking in another direction, perhaps at some distortion of the truth or some conveniently easy portion of the truth?

None so deaf

The third 'truth to tell' statement in verse 11 seems to suggest that Jesus interprets this reaction as intentional dullness; that possibly it is not so much that Nicodemus (and certainly the other teachers) cannot understand as that they *will not* understand. There are none so deaf as those who won't hear! We need to be willing to go back to the beginning, back to basics, to be 'born again' into a spiritual understanding, if we are ever to enter the Kingdom of God.

The truth about regeneration is comparatively 'down-to-earth' teaching about clearly verifiable fact, even if it is spiritual fact, yet they cannot or will not believe it (3:11). How will they ever believe what he tells them about heavenly things unless they accept this first basic truth of spiritual understanding? How will we believe in heavenly things if we do not allow ourselves to undergo this basic spiritual experience, for, after all, nobody has ever 'come back to tell us what it's like' in the life beyond (3:12, 13)? Yet Jesus does go on, he must go on, to tell them of such things—of crucifixion and eternal life, of salvation and judgment, the judgment of light and darkness (3:14-21).

The truth about regeneration is the primary truth. It is not the whole truth but it is the basic experience from which all spiritual growth originates, and from which all other spiritual truth emerges. Only when the Spirit is a living, breathing reality within us can we hope to become conversant with all the truth of the spiritual realm.

2. THE TRUTH ABOUT JESUS' AUTHORITY
(John 5:19-47)

'I am telling you the truth: the Son can do nothing on his own; he does only what he sees his Father doing, What the Father does, the Son also does' (5:19).

'I am telling you the truth: whoever hears my words and believes in him who sent me has eternal life' (5:24).

'I am telling you the truth: the time is coming—the time has already come—when the dead will hear the voice of the Son of God, and those who hear it will come to life' (5:25).

AS with the third chapter, the fifth chapter also has a trilogy of 'truths to tell'—this time about Jesus' authority. Jesus has:

- (a) authority to represent the Father;
- (b) authority to give eternal life;
- (c) authority to bring about the resurrection of the dead.

One with the Father

First, he has authority to represent the Father on earth: 'The Son can do nothing on his own; he does only what he sees his Father doing' (5:19). They are united in their action. Just two verses earlier (5:17) Jesus had said: 'My Father is always working, and I too must work.' Commenting on this picture of a working-class God and Saviour, Charles S. Duthie writes:

> The God who has always been at work and still is at work in his world is the God who forms the delicate snowflake and nourishes the giant oak into mature strength and holds the unnumbered galaxies in the hollow of his hand. His might is the might of one who has shown us in Jesus Christ how much he cares for each of his children. This working God is represented by a working Son, a Saviour who does the same work as the Father.

This does *not* mean that Jesus has no identity or authority of his own. Scripture tells us: 'Not one thing in all creation was made without him' (John 1:3); 'God put *all* things under his feet' (1 Corinthians 15:27).

What it does mean is that Jesus and the Father are so at one in nature and purpose that they inevitably think and act the same. They are never in conflict. But if Jesus, who is 'co-equal in power and glory' with the Father, could not act or teach or judge or just *be* without being conscious that he was doing it all as the Father would do it, should we not, all the more, seek to live life as a splendid *pas de deux* with God?

To change the metaphor, we should seek to be a mirror image of Jesus. 'Imitation is the sincerest form of flattery,' says the proverb. Genuine imitation is also the sincerest form of worship. Just as the little boy with toy cornet stands beside his father as he plays the real thing, and gazes out of the corner of his eye so that he may reproduce as exactly as possible his father's actions, so we must keep an eye on God continually if we hope to learn to be like him.

Nevertheless, the word 'imitation' is not always used in a pleasant connotation. 'Beware of imitations,' we are sometimes warned, referring to goods that seem like the real thing but aren't. The little boy sitting next to his dad in the Army band may get his father's actions off to a T, but the toy cornet's 'music' gives the game away. Frederick Coutts wrote of this kind of imitation: 'Likeness to Christ is no affair of external imitation. . . . Holiness does not begin with an outward conformity of habit but with an inward receiving of the Spirit.' In *My fair lady*, Professor Higgins's attempt to pass off the dustman's daughter as a duchess failed because, as he said, it is 'not only *how* a girl pronounces, but *what* she pronounces' that matters. We need to *be* like Jesus, not just *seem* like him, just as he is like the Father.

When Jesus uttered this first truth about authority, it was in fact a response to an accusation which the Jewish authorities were making (5:18) that Jesus had broken the Sabbath, and claimed God as his Father, and thereby was claiming equality with God. So Jesus is agreeing that this *is* in fact what he is claiming. He is not playing down his authority but establishing it at the highest level.

Eternal life

Secondly, the truth is that Jesus has authority not just to represent the Father, but to act for him in his dealings with mankind (5:24). His authority will even extend to raising the dead (5:21), judging the world (5:22), and receiving equal honour with the Father (5:23). Specifically he can grant eternal life, which is quite clearly a prerogative of God. The one who hears Jesus' message and believes in him *has* eternal life and freedom from judgment. Note the present tense 'has'. It is a *fait accompli*, a foregone conclusion.

We do not only see what God is *like* in Jesus. His likeness to God, his task as judge, and his position of honour with the Father, could all just make him totally remote from us and from our needs. However, he shows us that God is a God of love, a God to whom we can turn with hope, rather than one from whom we turn in fear. We see that Jesus is the way through sin to salvation, through judgment to eternal life. He does not just show us what God is like; he acts out his love, his grace.

William Temple writes:

> If when we hear the Son we believe what the Father declared through him, that is in itself an entry into fellowship with God, and therefore involves eternal life. For this *is*—it does not *earn* but it *is*—eternal life (17:3). For such a one, judgment is over, the passage *out of death to life* is accomplished.

Jesus began his high-priestly prayer: 'Father, the hour has come. Give glory to your Son. . . . For you gave him authority over all mankind, so that he might give eternal life to all those you gave him. And eternal life means knowing you, the only true God, and knowing Jesus Christ, whom you sent' (17:1-3).

Resurrection and judgment

Thirdly, the truth is that Jesus has authority to bring about the resurrection of the dead for eternal life or for condemnation according to his judgment (5:25, 29). The statement that 'the time is coming—the time has already come' may seem confusing (see Key 7), but surely Jesus is just saying that the criterion for eternal life—both in this life and in the life to come—is the same. It is those who hear his words who will have life (5:24, 25).

Note too that Jesus says he has been given the right to judge (5:27) not because he is the Son of God, but because he is the Son of Man. He 'was tempted in every way that we are' (Hebrews 4:15), and it is from that position of knowledge that he passes judgment.

But all of this is in harmony with the Father's will (5:30) and Jesus is not just making these great claims for himself. He does not need proof for himself; he has the witness in himself—the proof of just knowing (5:34). But for others the truth is confirmed by five witnesses:

5:32-35	John the Baptist, whom they had accepted as a prophet;
5:36	the signs Jesus is doing—his deeds validate his words;

17

5:37, 38	the Father—if they would only listen to him;
5:39, 40	the Scriptures—which speak of Jesus;
5:45-47	the teaching of Moses.

But proof is only proof to those who will accept it as proof. As John Goldingay has written: 'One can never expect to prove that something is God's word. Recognising something as God's word is always and inevitably an act of spiritual discernment, an act of faith.' Men continually produce optical illusions for themselves by 'turning a blind eye'.

Jesus is no upstart healer. He is Son of God and sole agent of God, and therefore has authority to heal, and—even more staggering—to give eternal life, and to act as judge in this life and the next.

3. THE TRUTH ABOUT OUR VITALITY

(John 6:25-58)

'I am telling you the truth: you are looking for me because you ate the bread and had all you wanted, not because you understood my miracles' (6:26).

'I am telling you the truth. . . . What Moses gave you was not the bread from heaven. . . . For the bread that God gives is he who comes down from heaven and gives life to the world' (6:32, 33).

'I am telling you the truth: he who believes has eternal life' (6:47, 48).

'I am telling you the truth: if you do not eat the flesh of the Son of Man and drink his blood, you will not have life in yourselves' (6:53).

JOHN chapter 6 has four occurrences of the phrase, 'I am telling you the truth', and they are all about our spiritual vitality; about how we can experience the spiritual satisfaction of having the life of God within us. If chapter three speaks of spiritual birth then chapter six speaks of spiritual food, and spiritual growth and spiritual completion.

Material or spiritual

At the beginning of the chapter (6:1-14) we have the story of the miracle of the feeding of the crowd of 5,000. This made such an impact that Jesus was aware that the crowd would try to make him king (6:15), and so he evades them. The next day they manage to catch up with him (6:25). Immediately, he challenges them with the fact that they are there because they benefitted from the miracle, not because they understood it (6:26), and he tells them to look for the eternal, spiritual satisfactions which are available through the 'Son of Man' (6:27).

The people, then, had gone to great pains to find Jesus because of what he had done for them in the way of material benefits, rather than for what he revealed of God's nature, that is, for spiritual blessings. He insisted on the primacy of faith, of believing. Maturity of spiritual

19

understanding will mean that we are less concerned with the wonderful things God can do for us in material terms, than in what God can do for us in spiritual terms, what we can gain through personal communion with the Son of Man, on whom is God the Father's seal of approval (6:27). The first 'truth to tell', then, the first double 'verily' in this chapter, tells us that our greatest satisfactions and our greatest blessings will be spiritual not material.

The true bread is a person

With their minds still on the proliferation of five loaves among 5,000 people, the crowd asks Jesus to perform another such miracle (6:30) and compares yesterday's miracle with the provision of manna to the Israelites in the desert (6:31). Jesus almost dismisses this as irrelevant and says that the real 'bread of Heaven' which will 'feed us now and evermore' is a person (6:32, 33). Even now they show that they are only there for the bread, and ask for an everlasting supply of it: 'Give us free bread every day,' as *The Living Bible* puts it (6:34). So Jesus makes it even plainer, telling them that he is the bread of life, he is the source of all blessings and fulfilment (6:35). Everyone and anyone who 'makes a meal of' him will be satisfied and receive eternal life (6:37-40).

Even when they begin to grasp his meaning, they cannot accept the truth. If God's provision was a person, it would surely have to be a very special person, but they all know Jesus' ordinary origins (6:42). He didn't come down from the sky! So Jesus changes the wording in 6:46 from 'came down from Heaven' to 'who is from God'. Their criticism (6:41, 42) was an underestimation of who he was. They assumed they knew all there was to know about him, because they knew his earthly parents, but they ignored the fact that he also had a heavenly origin—he 'came down from Heaven', he was 'from God', and could not be adequately described in purely human terms. How often we judge by appearances and miss the main meaning!

Jesus could have *bought* their loyalty by making life 'an easy, smooth and pleasant path', but he is concerned to show them that life's real meaning is to be seen in terms of personality rather than prosperity, that life's real goal is spiritual development, rather than material acquisition.

Tell that to a starving man and you will not get much response, of course. His prior need is physical. That is why Jesus had fed the crowd the previous day. It is also one reason, in addition to the purely humanitarian one, why Christians should try to feed the world's starving millions. Until they get bread they cannot be expected to show an interest in the 'bread who is a person'. Salvation Army social services began because William Booth and his helpers quickly realised that the appalling temporal circumstances of a large number of people made their (spiritual) salvation most unlikely unless attention was given also to their material needs. We do need food, although our needs do not end there. As Frederick Buechner says, 'Man does not live by bread alone, but he also does not live long without it. To eat is to acknowledge our dependence—both on food and on each other. It also reminds us of other kinds of emptiness.'

Or it should do! But Christians have often found it very difficult, as Jesus was doing on that day following the hunger lunch, to move the people on to a realisation of their greater emptiness, their emptiness of soul. That is perhaps why he felt it wrong to repeat the meal now that the need was somewhat less pressing. How do you break the cycle of hunger, or the cycle of greed? How do you move people on from a dependence on daily soup runs or regular humanitarian air drops to an awareness of, and ability to meet, their own deepest needs? Only by presenting them with the person who is the bread that came down from Heaven.

So the second great 'truth to tell' in this chapter is that our eternal satisfactions will all be found in a person, that the Son of Man is the source of all spiritual blessings.

Here and hereafter

In the Greek New Testament the words for 'bread' or 'food' are used 17 times between 6:25 and 6:58, and 'from Heaven' 10 times. But we must also note that eternal life has eight references. The bread who is a person has all the ingredients which will sustain spiritual life, and not in this life only but also in the life hereafter. 'I am telling you the truth: he who believes has eternal life. I am the bread of life' (6:47, 48), but also 'If anyone eats this bread, he *will* live *for ever*' (6:51). Future tense as well as present!

The third truth about our spirituality, then, is that the sustenance received from the bread of life has no sell-by date. It relates to both the here and the hereafter, and it relates to the same quality of life sustained by the same 'bread' in both the present life and the life beyond. The trauma of physical death does not destroy or disrupt that life, but only deepens and enhances it. This life is 'age-long'—it goes on for ever.

> Thou art the bread that satisfies for ever,
>   The inward health that overcomes disease,
> The love that lives through death, subsiding never,
>   My secret fortress and my soul's release.
>
> (Catherine Baird,
> *The song book of The Salvation Army*, No 631)

The bread is flesh and blood

In 6:51-58 the metaphor changes. Jesus is not saying anything essentially different; he is just saying it in a different way. Instead of the symbolism of eating bread, he now uses the symbolism of eating meat and drinking blood—devouring the flesh and drinking the blood of the one who gives eternal life.

We must note that these are figures of speech. They are not a reference to sacramental rituals as we know them, but rather an illustration of sacramental reality—that a transfer of grace can take place between the one who is bread, or meat, or blood, from Heaven and the believer who has faith in him. In whatever way we *represent* the intake of all that is *embodied* in Jesus, we must remember that the *essential* sacrament is the reception of the 'Godness' which shows in the human personality of Jesus. The literal drinking of blood would, of course, have been even more repulsive to the Jews than to us (see Leviticus 3:17). For them 'drinking blood' must have had a wholly figurative meaning. But 'blood' symbolised life, so that drinking the blood of Jesus meant partaking of the life which Jesus made available.

So whatever symbols we use, or even if we use none, what matters is that we experience the infusion of life and strength which comes to us as a result of us knowing Christ within us, part of us. 'I am telling you the truth: if you do not eat the flesh of the Son of Man and drink his blood, you will not have life in yourselves' (6:53). The truth of our spirituality is that it comes from God's Son, but must be made part of us, and then it will last forever or at least as long as we allow it to.

> Spirit of God, thou art the bread of Heaven
> Come for my need in Jesus Christ the Lord;
> Broken in him whose life was freely given
> In deathless love he only could afford.

> (Catherine Baird,
> *The song book of The Salvation Army*, No 631)

4. THE TRUTH ABOUT OUR LIBERTY

(John 8:28-59)

'I am telling you the truth: everyone who sins is a slave of sin' (8:34).

'I am telling you the truth: whoever obeys my teaching will never die' (8:51).

'I am telling you the truth. . . . Before Abraham was born, "I Am"' (8:58).

THESE three great truths in chapter eight are more closely interlinked than at first may appear. They are all connected to a long-running argument which Jesus had, not with the hardened opposition of Jewish leaders who had no intention of heeding him, but with those who were predisposed to believe him, those who, as 8:31 tells us, 'believed in him'. And when we look back at 8:28 we see that what they accepted was the very big claim that Jesus made: 'I Am Who I Am'; in other words 'I am equal with the God whose name is "I Am Who I Am" ' (the name God gave for himself to Moses in Exodus 3:14). But they were unwilling to go a step further in the application of the truth. They were willing enough to accept Jesus' claims about himself, but not willing to see what that implied about themselves, about their own spiritual parentage.

Slavery to sin

So it is those who have already accepted the fact of his divinity who refuse at the next fence (8:32), who cannot accept what to us might seem a much less demanding truth, for when Jesus goes on to say 'the truth will make you free', immediately their religious and racial hackles rise. How can Jesus suggest that they are not free as it is? They are proud descendants of Abraham, members of God's chosen people. 'Make us free? We *are* free! Hebrews never, never, never shall be slaves!' (see 8:33). They are willing to accept that Jesus is God, that he is their saviour, but not that they need saving, not that they are in any kind of bondage. They are offered great blessings, but because of racial and religious pride, they are ready to cut off their nose to spite their face. So Jesus has to present them with one of his forceful truths: 'I am telling you the truth: everyone who sins is a slave of sin' (8:34), but 'if the Son sets you free, then you will be really free' (8:36). They are as slaves in the family, but the Son of the Father of the family can set them free to live as sons within the family.

He tells them that they are not true sons of Abraham because:

(a)   they reject the Son's teaching (8:37);
(b)   they do not follow Abraham's example (8:39);
(c)   they want to kill Jesus rather than listen to him (8:40).

So then they change tack and claim that it is God, not just Abraham, who is their Father, and they are his true sons (8:41). They think they will avoid criticism if they say 'We're all God's children', a phrase often used by those who wish to deny any kind of distinctive value judgements. But Jesus quickly retorts that if they were God's children they would love him because he came from God and his message is from God (8:42-43). 'He who comes from God listens to God's words. You, however, are not from God, and that is why you will not listen' (8:47).

Therefore, far from being God's sons or Abraham's sons, they are in fact sons of the devil, and that sonship is in fact slavery (8:44) and from that slavery only he, Jesus, can save them. We can be God's children by creation and Abraham's children by conception, but still the devil's children by choice. (Note that 'your father' in 8:41 must also be a reference to the devil, since they are acting neither as Abraham's children nor as God's children.) The truth about the devil is that he 'has never been on the side of truth' (8:44), whereas Jesus *is* the truth, he is the one who can say without fear of contradiction: 'I am telling you the truth'.

So the truth about their proud boasts of liberty is that they are in fact in bondage, in bondage to the devil.

Liberty in Christ

The reaction of these adversaries of Jesus to all this is to suggest that he must be a Samaritan, not really one of God's children at all in their eyes, a real outsider. And he must be demon-possessed into the bargain (8:48). Like the pot calling the kettle black, the Jews were dishonouring Christ by saying that he was possessed with the demon of self-importance. In fact he was just telling the truth, seeing he was the Son of God, and it would hardly have been God-honouring to tell a pack of lies about it! So Jesus calmly denies their allegation, and states that he is seeking no honour for himself ('Self-praise is no honour'), but that God has honoured him and so should they (8:49-50). He was doing the will of God and leaving his reputation with God.

William Barclay writes:

> The Jews believed they were religious people, but because they had clung to *their* idea of religion instead of to God's idea, they had drifted so far from God that they had become godless. They were in the terrible position of men who were *godlessly serving God*. One 'godlessly serves God' when the central figure is oneself (one's religious ideals, values, achievements, preoccupations) rather than God.

Liberty from sin and also liberty from any kind of religion which exalts self, and so denies God, is to be found in Jesus. That is the truth about our liberty.

Deliverance from death

'I am telling you the truth: whoever obeys my teaching will never die' (8:51). Still these reluctant believers find some other fault in what Jesus is saying, which is that his teaching gives freedom from death, brings eternal life. This is the ultimate arrogance on his part as far as they are concerned. Abraham died; the prophets died; so their religion has never promised immortality (8:52). Who does he think he is? Does he think he's better than Abraham?

We should remember that belief in life after death in Old Testament times was largely confined to a belief in Sheol, a misty underworld of spirits caught in a sort of never-ending half-life. In the time of Jesus, while Pharisees had some belief in the hereafter, other Jews, including the Sadducees, did not. Belief in life, therefore, life in all its fullness, is a Christian belief. It is not difficult, then, to see how revolutionary was the statement of Jesus: 'Whoever obeys my teaching will never die.'

But that is just what Jesus *is* gently claiming, while at the same time insisting that he is not seeking any honour which the Father has not already given him, and he is only obeying him (8:54, 55). Abraham 'saw Jesus coming' and was thrilled to bits (8:56). They resort to charging him with historical inaccuracy, pointing out that a youngster like him could not possibly have known Abraham (8:57). They are forgetting that they are not talking history but eternity. So Jesus has to point out the third great 'truth to tell' about liberty—that it is eternal, and he is eternal, that he was God before Abraham was even a twinkle in someone's eye: 'I am telling you the truth. . . . Before Abraham was born, "I Am" ' (8:58).

That was too much! They began to arm themselves to stone this blasphemer to death, but when they turned back to pelt him he was no longer there!

25

5. THE TRUTH ABOUT OUR SECURITY
(John 10:1-18)

'I am telling you the truth: the man who does not enter the sheepfold by the gate, but climbs in some other way, is a thief and a robber. The man who goes in through the gate is the shepherd of the sheep . . . I am the good shepherd' (10:1, 2, 11).

'I am telling you the truth: I am the gate for the sheep' (10:7).

HERE in chapter 10 we have two vivid pictures of the relationship of the shepherd and his sheep, pictures in which the Lord Jesus is to be identified as the Good Shepherd. This is true even when Jesus says, 'I am the gate for the sheep' or 'the door of the sheepfold' (10:7), for this was part of the shepherd's function as we shall see. He was a 'gate' or a 'door' as far as the security of the sheep was concerned. Jesus is thinking both of a door open to opportunity and of a door closed for protection.

First he speaks of the communal village fold where in winter all the village sheep were housed overnight under the care of a single door-keeper. In the morning the shepherds would enter, call their own sheep and lead them to pasture. Each man's sheep would know his voice and anyone entering by any other way, or giving a different call, would be recognisable as an imposter and thief.

Jesus does not gatecrash into the fold of our personality (10:2), but, with his gentle but easily recognised call, he invites us to fellowship, and following, and spiritual food (10:4). With the Good Shepherd we may safely 'go in and out and find pasture' (10:9) amid the dangers and temptations of the world.

Verses 7 to 10 refer to the summer fold on the hillside, a fold which consisted simply of a wall with an opening. The shepherd lay across this opening and was the door, so that any harm that came to the sheep came literally 'over his dead body'. If we live within the limits imposed by the shepherd-door we will be both satisfied and safe.

Just outside

Our security depends on us being on the inside of the fold. Just being in the vicinity isn't sufficient. Some years ago we were walking on the lower slopes of Ben Nevis and came upon the decaying carcass of an animal. We thought at first it might be a fox or other wild animal, but then we noticed some grey-white hair on a cloven hoof, and concluded that it must have been a sheep. It had succumbed to one of the dangers of the open mountainside, but what was most striking was that its remains lay within a few yards of a sheepfold. Had it been inside no doubt it would have been secure. Just outside, it was in as much danger as if it had been a mile away. So it is with the Kingdom of God. Inside, we know the security of the care of the Good Shepherd, over whose dead body any harm will come to us. Outside, even just outside, we risk losing his care.

Life in all its fullness

We might suppose that a good shepherd would be primarily concerned with the production of *good* meat and *good* wool, and not so much about the sheep having a *good* life. Yet this Good Shepherd says, 'I have come in order that you might have life—life in all its fullness' (10:10). He wants us to have not just the life that is the opposite of death, but the life that is 'real living', life at its best. To him we are not butcher-meat or pew-fodder—we are beloved individuals for whom he is willing to give his own life (10:15). We sometimes think of God as a spoilsport rather than a good sport, an interferer not an encourager, one who stifles rather than one who invigorates, one who takes away rather than one who completes. The picture of the Good Shepherd sets us right here—both he and his Father want us to have 'all the very best'.

Security in Christ

Verses 11-18 add other thoughts to our understanding of our security in Christ. First, Jesus is the Good Shepherd because he is willing to die for his sheep. Our security has a higher priority than his own (10:11-13, 17, 18). This is because the sheep are his own; he is part-owner (with the Father) as well as carer for the sheep. On the other hand, a 'hired hand' would be more likely to give priority to his own security. If there is danger, he will be the first to 'scatter', unheeding the 'crowd of frightened sheep'. He is ready to do a fair day's work for a fair day's pay, but getting killed into the bargain is not part of his contract!

Secondly, our security is individually assured (10:15) because the Good Shepherd knows his sheep. Jesus cares for us not just as one big flock, *en masse*, but as individuals. This is true even on a much smaller scale, with sparrows or hairs: 'Not one sparrow is forgotten by God. Even the hairs of your head have all been counted. So do not be afraid; you are worth much more than many sparrows!' (Luke 12:6, 7). If Jesus were teaching today, no doubt his examples would come from nuclear technology or astro-physics. If a computer can hold on one small disc a vast number of facts, how much easier it is to believe in a God who can hold us all in his mind.

Thirdly, while it is individual, our security is not exclusive (10:16). We have no proprietary rights over the Shepherd. We cannot say, 'You are ours, and no other sheep can lay claim to you.' His aim is not just to keep us safe, but to call *others* who will hear his voice, and incorporate them all ultimately into one flock. This statement about 'other sheep' is sometimes used to suggest that other religions have equal validity with Christianity. For Jesus, however, 'this fold' no doubt meant Judaism, and 'other sheep' signified the Gentiles. But even if he *were* talking of other religions, Jesus' point is that all the flocks will become one flock. It is not a case of 'many flocks, one shepherd', but finally 'one flock, one shepherd'.

We are 'of the flock' when we recognise and obey the Shepherd's voice. A great actor was once asked to recite Psalm 23 at a public function. He did so with all the technique he could summon and the crowd acclaimed him. Next, an old minister read the same psalm, and his rendering was met with an awed silence. Explaining the difference, the actor was gracious enough to say, 'I knew the psalm; he knew the Shepherd.' Our ultimate security lies in knowing the Good Shepherd.

6. THE TRUTH ABOUT OUR EXPENDABILITY
(John 12:20-36)

'I am telling you the truth: a grain of wheat remains no more than a single grain unless it is dropped into the ground and dies. If it does die, then it produces many grains' (12:24).

THIS single 'truth to tell' in John chapter 12 seems to be rather a *non sequitur*—it does not clearly arise from what goes before. Some Jews approach Philip (a disciple with a Greek name) wanting an introduction to Jesus. He shares the request with Andrew, the only other Greek-named disciple, but one closer to Jesus. Does this not suggest that we are not all equally qualified to meet the seeker's every need? We may be the type whom people feel they can easily approach, but we may have to pass them on to someone differently qualified if they are to come close to Jesus. Teamwork is needed in evangelism.

It is significant that, as the net of official opposition closes in on Jesus, and as those Jews who at first lauded him for his miraculous powers drift away to save their own skins (or even just their own faces), there comes this small group of Greeks (ie Gentiles), who want to speak to Jesus. Will he see them? He had not ministered to the Gentiles (Matthew 15:24); he had not sent his disciples to them (Matthew 10:5, 6). But here he seems to respond to their approach as a sign of the widened ministry of the cross that will include all men. Though the passage does not say explicitly that he did see them, it makes best sense if we assume that he did, and that verses 23-26 are his direct message to them. So that they are under no misapprehension, Jesus gives a stronger statement than ever of his purposes. Though he begins with a suggestion that he (the Son of Man) is about to receive great glory, he makes it plain that that glory will come through death. The secret of spiritual success is expendability. The true servant must be ready to walk the way of the cross. But 'the cross will turn to glory' (12:23). As William Temple summarises it: 'Self-love is self-destruction; self-centredness is sin; and self-love is hell.'

God's arithmetic

We must realise that God's arithmetic is sometimes different from ours. If we let a grain of wheat = 1, and the ground (worthless dust) = 0, then according to our arithmetic 1-0 = 1.

So, if you have a grain of wheat and you *do not* put it in the dust of the earth it stays a single grain. God's arithmetic agrees with our arithmetic there.

But if we make a second equation on the basis of *adding* the grain to the dust of the earth, that is when God's arithmetic differs from ours. We would say that 1+0 = 1, but God's arithmetic achieves the equation 1+0 = 30, or 60, or perhaps 100 (Mark 4:8); one grain apparently thrown away may produce 30 or 60 or even 100 grains. The secret of fruitfulness is in our understanding, and accepting, our expendability.

A complementary truth to emerge from this verse is that in God's economy 'little things mean a lot', and if we contribute what we can, he will multiply it, and he can make a lot out of a little.

Dr A. W. Carlisle writes:

> Most people seeing a cornfield teeming with golden harvest would think: 'What a picture of life in all its fullness! What a complete contrast to death in all its emptiness!' The God of all wisdom sees much deeper. The abundant harvest is eloquent testimony to the potency of death. . . . Yes, the way to fruitfulness lies through death. The seed committed to the earth suffers a separation of its parts before it can germinate.

The right track

The principles outlined for the Greeks in verses 24-26 seem to be amplified for the Jews in the succeeding verses. The audience is referred to in verses 29 and 34 as 'the crowd' and the latter verse refers to 'our Law', so the crowd referred to must be Jews. Jesus says that though self-sacrifice to the point of death is naturally abhorrent (12:27), it is the whole point of his existence ('that is why I came') and a heavenly voice confirms that his whole life is glorifying God (12:28b). He is on the right track!

Jesus' next statement, however, is that that track leads to a cross. He will be 'lifted up' (12:32), an ambiguous phrase to us, perhaps, but not to the crowd (12:33, 34). He will be crucified. Though they understand his meaning, they do not understand why this should happen to him. They have been coming to believe that Jesus is the Messiah, but now he speaks of crucifixion. The Scriptures, however, said that the Messiah would live for ever! Their laboured efforts to put two and two together did not produce the answer they expected. Then they remembered (12:34) that Jesus had spoken of himself as the Son of

Man (3:14). Was the Son of Man who would die perhaps different from the Messiah who would live for ever? They could not conceive of a crucified Messiah, so they would not believe that God could conceive of it either. If Jesus was to be crucified he could not be the Messiah.

The trouble was that they were thinking of death as the end. Their equation omitted one of the factors involved—that there could be life and influence beyond death—so they could not get the right answer. The vital truth which Jesus had expounded in 12:24 has to be fed into the equation of the life of Jesus before it can make any sense, and that vital truth is the truth of expendability. Only when the seed is sown *and dies* can it bring forth fruit, and not just an equal amount of grain to what is sown, but thirty-fold, sixty-fold or even one-hundred-fold.

As Dr H. F. Lovell Cocks has written:

> The gate into the Kingdom is a narrow one. The would-be disciple must be ready to forsake all for the sake of the Kingdom. ... 'Loving' and 'hating' here [12:25] ... refer not to our feelings but to our priorities. To 'love' our life is to put ourselves first. It is to be primarily concerned with our own safety, our own comfort, our own standing among men. To 'hate' our life does not mean that we care nothing for our safety, comfort, popularity, and the rest—but that these things, wherever they come in our scale of priorities, never come first. What comes first is God's Kingdom—God's will and our obedience to it.

And what is true for Jesus is true for the Jews, and the Greeks, and us! It is in this sense that we need to learn the truth of our expendability.

7. THE TRUTH ABOUT OUR HUMILITY

(John 13:1-17)

'I am telling you the truth: no slave is greater than his master, and no messenger is greater than the one who sent him' (13:16).

A late-night briefing

IN the next few sections we shall look at a special segment of John's Gospel—the 'last supper' discourse of Jesus with his disciples (chapters 13 to 16). As Albert Orsborn's song says:

> In the secret of [his] presence . . .
> The Lord will come, revealing
> All the secrets of his ways.

> (*The song book of The Salvation Army*, No 591)

What 'secrets of his ways' did he tell to these men who had been so close to him, in that last-minute, late-night briefing? What were the main truths to be passed on to those disciples on whom would depend the survival and future spread of his message?

As we have already seen, John's Gospel is a very well organised document, arranged carefully so as to reveal the key ideas and priorities in the teaching of Jesus. Sometimes it almost looks as if John is telling the story in such a way as to bring out important truths that he thought the other three Gospels did not emphasise strongly enough. It is especially interesting that, while the first 12 chapters deal with the three years of the public ministry, most of the second half of the book (chapters 13-21) deals with just three days or a little more, the long weekend from Thursday evening to Sunday morning at the end of his life. So John gives us much more detail about Christ's last hours and last words than about anything else and much more about these last things than does any of the other three Gospel-writers.

Readiness to receive

The washing of the disciples' feet was a *sacrament*—a sharing of grace through the medium of something material or some external act.

But Jesus also made it a most powerful *sermon,* the main point of which was twofold: not *just* what he *could* do for them, but what they *should* do for *each other.*

The first impact of this staggering blueprint for the ministry of the helping hand was to show his own humility, his preparedness to serve even those who ought to have been serving him. We ought to come to Christ knowing that he wants to serve us, and *ready to receive*, willing to receive what he has to give us, even when we do not deserve it, even when we are tempted, like Peter, to be proud and defiant and self-sufficient, even when we might think we are quite capable of doing the needful for ourselves or for each other. We must be ready to receive the sacrament of ministry at the Saviour's hand. Whether or not he 'should', by conventional standards, be doing it or not, Jesus is ready to cleanse and bless us. Are we going to place predetermined limits on how far we are going to let Jesus bless us?

William Temple writes:

> The divine humility shows itself in rendering service . . . 'The Son of Man came not to receive service but to give it' (Mark 10:45). But man's humility does not begin with the giving of service; it begins with the readiness to receive it. For there can be much pride and condescension in our giving of service. . . . So man's humility shows itself first in the readiness to receive service from our fellow-men and supremely from God.

Humility is being willing first to receive. Peter said at first, 'Not me! Not likely!' If he hadn't repented, if he hadn't abandoned his proud refusal to receive, to accept, he would have found himself isolated from the Master for ever. Commenting on some 'superior' people, T. R. Glover said: 'They thought they were being religious when they were merely being fastidious.' Peter's fastidious concern for the proprieties almost cut him off from the source of blessing.

So, when we come into the Saviour's presence, do we come with attitudes at one or the other extreme of Peter's massive pendulum swing? First he says: 'Never at any time will you wash my feet!' (13:8). (Bless me if you can!) But then, at the other extreme, he blurts out: 'Do not wash only my feet, then! Wash my hands and head, too!' (13:9). (Bless me so much that I won't have to do anything for myself!) Jesus is waiting to bless, if we will let him. He can minister to our most mundane need and our deepest spiritual condition.

Willingness to serve

The equally important truth which comes at the end of this passage is, however, 'You, then, should wash one another's feet' (13:14). The ministry of Jesus does not let us off the hook of responsibility for each other. It does not let us off the hook of responsibility for what happens when we meet together in the Lord's presence. Jesus tells the disciples that their responsibility is the same as his, that they ought to do what he has just done. The *Authorised Version* makes it even clearer: 'If *I* then, your Lord and Master, have washed your feet; ye also ought to wash one another's feet.' We have the same responsibility for ministry as does our Lord. The only possible difference is that there is no unwillingness on his part to meet our needs, whereas we may well hesitate about playing our part. But we all have the same shared responsibility for ministry: 'You have to wash one another's feet; you have to meet each other's needs.'

Just as the Master does not place any disciple's responsibility as *higher* than another's, so he does not place any disciple's responsibility as being any *less* than *his own*.

We may ask ourselves why none of them did the needful. Why did nobody take over, even when they saw Jesus doing the unthinkable? Why do we sometimes fail to accept the ministry of service?

(a) Perhaps the disciples didn't see the need because they weren't looking.

(b) Perhaps they argued, 'It's beneath me. Oh, yes, I know it's beneath Jesus too. He shouldn't have to do it, but it's not my fault if there isn't a servant to do it. Who made the arrangements? Let *them* make up for any deficiency. *They* should have made sure the toilet facilities were all right. I can't be expected to do anything about it.'

(c) Perhaps they said, 'I suppose I could do it, but there are eleven others on a par with me. Why should I be the odd one out?'

(d) Perhaps they said, 'Well Jesus can do it far better than I. It will be far more meaningful if he does it, so let him get on with it!'

(e) Perhaps they said, 'I've got more important things on my mind. For example, who's going to be the next leader if Jesus gets himself killed? It wouldn't do to be seen doing the lowly task now, just when a leadership struggle is beginning. I must keep a high profile, not get lost from sight by doing the servant's work!' Luke tells us that they had just been arguing about who was greatest (22:24-27).

It wasn't that Jesus was trying to be on a par with the disciples in any kind of false chumminess, or that he was trying to evade a leader's responsibility. In the J. B. Phillips translation, 13:3 says: 'Jesus, with the full knowledge that the Father had put everything in his hands, and that he had come from God and was going to God, got up . . . and began to wash the disciples' feet.' He was acting from a *position of strength*, but that enabled him to adopt a *posture of lowliness*. He knew that he operated from a *base of privilege*, but he chose the *baseness* of a servant's role. The truly strong man stoops low to lift the heaviest burdens; the man of privilege shows his greatness by service. William Barclay says: 'The world is full of people who are standing on their dignity when they ought to be kneeling at the feet of their brethren.'

Jesus was aware too that 'he was going to God'. He might well have said, 'I won't be in this situation much longer! I'm going up higher.' But Jesus *did* what the Son of Man *had to do*. Do we ever avoid the costly or the difficult on the assumption that 'It'll last my time! I won't be here all that long. Let somebody else sort it out. Why should I get involved?'

Our shared responsibility for ministry never ceases. Jesus carried it out to the last.

By putting himself in the lowest position, Jesus made it impossible for any of his followers to claim any higher position. We can only be his disciples by kneeling as low as he. If the Master is servant, then we are all servants. By taking that position he ensured that an attitude of humility is the only proper posture for us.

Humility, then, is a willingness to give, a willingness to serve, as well as a willingness to receive. There is a well-known story about Salvation Army Cadet Samuel Logan Brengle. 'Brengle had once dreamed of being a bishop. He was a Methodist minister, but left a fine pastorate to join Booth's Salvation Army. But at first Booth accepted his services reluctantly and grudgingly. Booth said to Brengle, "You've been your own boss too long!" And in order to instil humility into Brengle, he set him to work cleaning the boots of the other trainees. And Brengle said to himself, "Have I followed my own fancy across the Atlantic in order to black boots?" And then as in a vision he saw Jesus bending over the feet of the rough unlettered fishermen. "Lord", he whispered, "You washed their feet; I will black their boots"' (Richard Collier: *The General next to God*).

Our shared responsibility is to share in ministry, in humility; that humility must make it possible to receive, as well as to serve.

8. THE TRUTH ABOUT OUR IDENTITY

(John 13:18-20)

'I am telling you the truth: whoever receives anyone I send receives me also; and whoever receives me receives him who sent me' (13:20).

THE disciples were to be identified with Christ in his mission of identifying God and identifying men with God. People might not be able to see God the Father, but while Jesus was in the flesh they had been able to see him, and so see God. 'Whoever has seen me has seen the Father' (14:9). And now that Jesus was no longer to be visible, people would have to see his personality, and so the Father's reality, in the lives of the disciples. What are the implications of this chain of identity, this identity bracelet—the Son identified with the Father, and the disciples identified with the Father through the Son?

First, it gives us a sense of real privilege. We are the representatives of Christ and so of the Father. As their ambassadors we are crucially involved in the advance of the Kingdom. Receiving us is like receiving the Trinity. Response to us is response to God the Father, Son and Holy Spirit.

Responsibility

But, secondly, like many privileges, this brings a sense of terrifying responsibility. If we don't look like God, people won't see him. If it doesn't happen in us and through us, it doesn't happen at all. We are responsible for people's knowledge of God. Think of an ambassador to an unfriendly country. In these days his position can mean tension, fear, isolation, disruption, disappointment, but, whatever the situation, his great responsibility is to *represent*. If our identity doesn't identify us with God's identity, then not only we but all who look to us will be unable to know him.

But notice that the first initiative does not lie with us. Note the words 'anyone I send' and 'who sent me' (13:20). We are engaged in

36

mission and the Greek verb from which mission comes means 'to send'. We can represent God because we are 'sent'. We cannot set *ourselves* up as representatives of Christ who is the expression, the revelation of God. We have to be *sent* before we can *represent*.

William Barclay says that the disciples were to be:

> Nothing less than the representatives of God himself. An ambassador does not go out as a private individual, armed with only his own personal qualities and qualifications. He goes out with all the glory and honour of his country upon him. To listen to him is to listen to his country; to honour him is to honour the country he represents; to welcome him is to welcome the ruler who sent him out. The great honour and the great responsibility of being a pledged Christian is that we stand in the world for Jesus Christ. We speak for him; we act for him. The honour of the Eternal is in our hands.

The truth, then, about our identity as Christians, as disciples, as ambassadors, is that we are identified with Christ, identified with the Master, and thus identified with the Father. That has its sense of privilege, but let us not be too carried away with that. It is much outweighed by the responsibilities of our status. We are a means to God's end. The important thing is not that people receive us well, but that through us they receive the Master, the one who sent us.

Representatives

In one sense, who we are doesn't matter nearly as much as whom we *represent,* though that is not to say that Christ has no use for our personality or that we should suppress our true identity. We are not just to be clones of a single personality. The remarkable thing is that Christ can be seen in each one of a limitless number of Christians. Whatever the variations in our appearance or the characteristics of our personality, once we are redeemed Christ can be seen in all of us. There can be a spiritual 'likeness' to Christ in us all, without us being carbon copies of each other. We all have our own 'fingerprints', our own personality profile, but we are all of the same 'species'—all Christians.

We can be just the one he needs to represent him in a specific situation. Not just anybody will do as an ambassador. We are handpicked to represent him in a particular place.

The Father had sent him. He was sending them. He is sending us.

They were to be links in a chain of spiritual privilege and responsibility. And, to tell you the truth, we are Christ's representatives just as he is God's representation in human form.

Agents

Another facet of this truth of identification with the Father is presented when we look at the corresponding saying in some of the other Gospels. For example, in Mark 9:36, 37 it is linked with the famous occasion when Jesus 'took a child and made him stand in front of them'. The wording there is: 'Whoever welcomes in my name one of these children, welcomes me; and whoever welcomes me, welcomes not only me but also the one who sent me.' We are his agents.

So while in one sense our identification with the Father brings us great honour as we become his representatives, in another sense it identifies us with the lowly and the humble.

William Barclay writes:

> A child has no influence at all; a child cannot advance a man's career nor enhance his prestige; a child cannot give us things. . . . A child needs things; a child must have things done for him. So Jesus says, 'If a man welcomes the poor, ordinary people . . . who have no influence and no wealth and no power, the people who need things done for them, he is welcoming me. More than that he is welcoming God.

Thus the identity bracelet that binds us together with Jesus and with God the Father also binds us to the childlike and the needy. The fact that we are God's representatives is not an honour that removes us from the common people, but a privilege that identifies us with the poor and the lowly, for 'whenever you did this for one of the least important of these brothers of mine, you did it for me!' (Matthew 25:40).

9. THE TRUTH ABOUT OUR LOYALTY
(John 13:21-30)

'I am telling you the truth: one of you is going to betray me' (13:21).

NOTE that there is no blanket condemnation here of all the disciples. They had *all* failed to meet the need of Jesus. They had *all* failed to meet each other's needs. They had *all* failed in their responsibilities. They had *all* been misguided in their motives and mistaken in their opinions. It seemed they had got it all wrong. But they were loyal and so there was hope for all of them—except one.

For Jesus knew them well enough ('I know those I have chosen' 13:18) to know that the loyalty didn't extend to all of them. He quoted a verse from the Psalms: 'Even my best friend, the one I trusted most, the one who shared my food, has turned against me' (41:9).

The bond of hospitality

In the Middle East, to eat bread with anybody was a sign of friendship and loyalty and created a sacred bond between the two. Exchanging hospitality in some parts of that area is still almost like becoming blood-brothers. Once hospitality has been given it must be maintained even if the two parties later find themselves to be from opposing camps.

Jesus and Judas had shared much more than bread, but that alone should have ensured Judas's loyalty.

Judas shows us that even the chosen can betray Christ. We are the chosen. Do we ever deliberately turn against him? Do we 'bite the hand that feeds us', as the quotation above from the Psalms suggests? Do we betray him with our lips and by our actions too?

The betrayer

Jesus knew them well enough to know that one would betray him, but his knowledge did not cause the betrayal. Jesus discerned what was in Judas's heart but he did not predestine his betrayal. No doubt all the

39

Twelve shifted uneasily under the accusation, 'One of you is going to betray me', but the eleven, however uneasy they felt, must have been aware of their own loyalty, however fragile. But Judas must have known immediately that it was him who was the betrayer.

We may wonder why Jesus did not say it straight out, why he did not immediately put the others out of their misery; why he didn't put his cards on the table; why, instead, he took something from the table—a piece of bread—and dipped it in the fondue dish and gave it to the Judas who came from Kerioth.

It was no 'eeny meeny meiny mo' selection designed to heighten the tension. And it does not seem to have been just a silent signal to Judas, an attempt to keep the truth from the others, although 13:29 shows that they did not really understand what was happening, thinking that his duties as treasurer demanded attention. Perhaps some of them would have tried to stop Judas forcibly if they had understood. But Jesus' action was in response to a clear question 'Who is it, Lord?' and he made a clear statement that he would give to the betrayer the bread that he had 'dunked' in the sauce.

We can only assume that Jesus used the little ritual to say the unsayable. He was so deeply troubled, so full of frustrated love for Judas, that he choked on his name; he literally could not bring himself to utter the name of the one who would betray him.

Even that did not make the betrayal inevitable. But 13:30 makes it much more certain: 'Judas accepted the bread.' Even then he could have repented of the ultimate act of disloyalty and turned back. But he went through with it, despite the fact that Jesus brought the issue out into the open and made very sure he knew what he was doing.

The ultimate night

'It was night' (13:30). Are we ever in danger of the ultimate night of being disloyal to him who has fed our souls, filled our minds, and offered us fulfilment? Note that it was a question of personal disloyalty to Christ. It wasn't that Judas was resigning his commission as treasurer, or withdrawing from the company of twelve disciples, or being unfair or untrue to his mates. It was his personal loyalty to Christ and to truth that was at stake. We are not talking of any pseudo-loyalty which a movement or an individual may seek to make supreme in our lives, or a loyalty which may be demanded of us but which may in fact conflict with our loyalty to Christ. It was his fundamental stance in relation to his Lord which was in question.

Loyalty can, in fact, be the very devil when it is misplaced loyalty. The Pharisees were loyal to a tradition. The scribes were loyal to a code of rules and regulations. The Saduccees were loyal to a doctrine. The Romans were loyal to a philosophy of government. Perhaps even

40

Judas was loyal to a set of false assumptions and distorted priorities. *But they were all against Christ.*

The minimum essential loyalty was once summed up by a Salvation Army leader in the words, 'Never bore holes in the ship you are travelling in', but even that ship may have been commandeered and be travelling in quite the wrong direction. Our basic loyalty is not to the ship but to the captain, not to a denomination but to a person.

Polycarp facing martyrdom said, 'Eighty-six years have I been his servant, and he has done me no wrong. How can I blaspheme my King who saved me?' The truth about our loyalty must be that it is a personal loyalty to Christ and to the truth of God which he embodies. There is no other loyalty for the Christian. If we lose that we lose all, as Judas soon realised to his cost. The tragedy is that he realised it after, rather than before, the dreadful act, and so seemed to leave himself no option but the ultimate folly of self-destruction.

We should grieve for any in our fellowship who have unobtrusively or obviously betrayed Christ or may do so in the future. Let us seek their restoration, for the truth is that even Judas's betrayal was made final only by his own suicide.

And let us remember that we are under the spotlight of the Master's knowledge of us. Our mistakes and our denials could so easily become our betrayals. There is a fine line between preventable error and deliberate disloyalty and the truth about Judas was that he had gone over that line, and failed to retrace his steps.

10. THE TRUTH ABOUT OUR HUMANITY

(John 13:31-36)

'I tell you now what I told the Jewish authorities, "You cannot go where I am going" ' (13:33).

JESUS here makes the same declaration twice to the disciples: 'I tell you . . . you cannot go where I am going' (13:33, 36). We must conclude that he is not talking about Gethsemane—they could go there, and did go there, later the same night, even if they could not share his agony. Nor is he talking about the High Priest's house or Herod's palace or Pilate's castle or even Golgotha. Some of them followed him there though they did not dare to identify with Jesus. Nor is he telling them that they cannot follow him to the cross. They could have chosen to share that form of death if they wanted to and some of them eventually did.

He must mean that they could not follow him through resurrection into the eternal world. He alone of them had the ability to escape into eternity at will *and to return.*

The strange thing about this passage is that Jesus aligns the disciples with the Jewish authorities (13:33). He's only telling them what he has already told the Pharisees and the chief priests. This seems to be a clear reference back to John 7:32-36 where he tells those groups when they try to arrest him: 'You will look for me, but you will not find me, because you cannot go where I will be' (7:34). They speculated whether he was going to flee the country and join the *diaspora*, the Jews who lived abroad as political or economic refugees in the Greek city states and elsewhere. What he really meant, of course, was that even when they did arrest him, even when he was crucified, he would not really be within their jurisdiction; they could not hold his spirit. He would escape to eternity.

Love in community

But if we cannot follow Jesus in that sense because our humanity, our finity, fences us in, Jesus does tell us, as he told the disciples, something that we can do. If we desire to be as near him as possible,

42

if we desire to live our human life at its best, if we desire to make our earthly state as near as possible to his heavenly state, we must live in loving community: 'And now I give you a new commandment: love one another' (13:34). John Gray writes:

> It is not an emotion Christ asks. Emotions are notoriously impossible to command. What he asks is that by a conscious and deliberate act we should set aside our own interests, willingly sacrifice for others and constantly make the effort to understand their point of view, and that we should do this, not now and again, but steadily and invariably. It is not easy to love even one person thus all the time, far less all whom we meet.

If we desire to be like him, if we desire to prepare for an eternity with him, this is the way we can do it.

Even if we are restricted by the confines of our humanity, even if we cannot for the present escape into the infinite world of eternity, we can live the life of Christ in the here and now; live the life of love; live the life of eternity; live it in community. As the song puts it, we can have a 'Heaven below'. We do not have the right to choose when and whether we enter the life above. It is the gift of Jesus, but meanwhile we can live the life of Jesus, live in the light of this new commandment he gave, live in the spirit he lived by—and if we do that, then that life of love will prepare us for our eternal destiny and 'everyone will know that you are my disciples' (13:35). David Richardson says: 'Jesus defines, or redefines, what humanity can be. He restores the broken image. Man is seen again as being in the image and likeness of God.'

A temporary restriction

But it is worth noting that when Jesus says the second time: 'You cannot go where I am going' (13:36) he adds something very significant: 'You cannot follow me *now* . . . but *later* you will follow me.'

This may be a particular word to Peter, foretelling his martyrdom, or it may be a general word to all disciples, foreseeing their eternal destiny. It may indeed be both. If it is the latter then the truth about our humanity is that though we are temporarily restricted by its limitations now, in this life, if we live out our humanity in community, if we love each other as he has loved us, we will eventually escape from this temporary humanity into eternity.

Frederick Buechner writes:

> Eternity is not endless time or the opposite of time. It is the essence of time. . . . Inhabitants of time that we are, we stand . . . with one foot in eternity.

There is a 'later' version of abundant life, as well as a 'now' version. They are *in essence* the same, but entry into the 'later' experience depends upon living the 'now' experience.

To quote Buechner again:

> We think of eternal life, if we think of it at all, as what happens when life ends. We would do better to think of it as what happens when life begins.

We have noticed Jesus using the words 'now' and 'later'. This is another of the minor verbal characteristics which run through these chapters. Jesus has already had cause to say to Peter more than once, 'Not now!', almost as a parent has to say it to an impatient child. The child wants a toy in a shop window display 'now'. He must have the attention of the parent 'now', however important the task that the parent is engaged with. He must have sweets or a biscuit 'now', and no amount of promises for 'afterwards' will suffice. For the child 'tomorrow', 'next week', 'next year' are meaningless terms, beyond his vision, beyond the reach of his grasping hand. In fact, one of the marks of developing adulthood is surely the willingness to wait, to work towards things, to look at things in the long term. Indeed we may even come to like the sound of 'tomorrow', '*mañana*', when it excuses us from difficult action. And we are told that with God 'a thousand years . . . are like one day' (Psalm 90:4). Perhaps, then, the willingness to wait is a sign of ultimate maturity.

Now is not always

But Peter is still the impatient child, spiritually. He wants it all now. And Jesus has already said to him and the other disciples:

> 'You do not understand *now* what I am doing, but you will understand *later*' (13:7).
> 'I tell you this *now* . . . so that when it *does happen*, you *will* believe' (13:19).

And we may look at several other instances of this 'Not now . . . later' kind of thinking in the teaching of Jesus, in fact a series of six promises, which show the disciples that this is a crisis point in their relationship with Jesus, a turning point, but in fact only a temporary stage. They include:

1. The promise of an eternal home: 'After I go and prepare a place for you, *I will come back* and take you to myself, so that you will be where I am' (14:3).

2. The promise of eternal vision: 'When I go, you will not be left all alone; *I will come back* to you. *In a little while* the world will see

44

me no more, but you will see me; and because I live, you also will live' (14:18).

3. The promise of an eternal presence: 'Whoever loves me will obey my teaching. My Father will love him, and *my Father and I will come to him* and live with him' (14:23).

4 . The promise of eternal joy: 'You heard me say to you, "I am leaving, but *I will come back to you.*" If you loved me, you would be glad that I am going to the Father; for he is greater than I' (14:28).

5. The promise of ultimate meaning: '*In a little while* you will not see me any more, and then *a little while later* you will see me' (16:16).

6. The promise of newness of life: 'Your sadness will turn into gladness' (16:20). Jesus then explains this with the analogy of a woman giving birth (16:21).

How sad that the disciples were too blind to take in the full import of these promises! 'What does this a *little while* mean?' they quibbled (16:18).

But the truth about our humanity, our frailty, is that though it prevents us leaving the confines of our earthly existence, it is a life of developing spiritual maturity and is a preparation for that life of eternity which Jesus promised us.

11. THE TRUTH ABOUT OUR FALLIBILITY
(John 13:37-38)

'I am telling you the truth: before the cock crows you will say three times that you do not know me' (13:38).

WE have seen in the last chapter that our humanity is finite, is limited, in that we are creatures of space and time. Jesus goes on to show Peter that he is also limited in courage and spiritual strength. There is much that we cannot understand now. That is the measure of our frailty, our fallibility. There is much that we cannot manage now. That is a measure of our weakness. But we can grow wiser; we can grow stronger by the ministry of the Spirit.

Peter has made the extravagant gesture of saying, 'I am ready to die for you!' (13:37), which shows quite clearly that he isn't ready! Often those who push themselves forward for position in the Church and elsewhere are the wrong people. It would be better if they had a measure of hesitation about their fitness for such responsibilities. So Jesus takes up Peter's statement and flings it back at him: 'Are you really ready to die?' (13:38). And he shows how empty the promise is by predicting Peter's desperate threefold denial that he had ever had anything to do with Jesus. None of the disciples was yet ready for martyrdom; none, not even Peter, was strong enough to follow Jesus to Calvary, let alone to eternal glory. So he had to be told firmly: 'Not now!' Joseph Parker says: 'There cannot be an *afterwards* of revelation, unless there is a *now* of obedience.'

So what was the difference between Peter and Judas? Was Peter any better than the one who had already decided to betray Jesus, if he himself was going to *deny* Jesus three times over. The difference was, perhaps, that Judas's betrayal was deliberate. It was premeditated. It was calculated. Peter's denial, on the other hand, was done in the heat of the moment, in a moment of weakness. He was so confused and afraid that he hardly knew what he was doing. He would never have believed it possible! He loved Jesus greatly, yet the truth about his humanity, the truth about his frailty was that despite his love, despite his promises, despite his protestations, he collapsed like a house of

46

cards at the first sign of personal danger, the first pressure of temptation. But he never meant it!

Yet it was still tragedy. Some of our worst betrayals can take place immediately after our most ardent protestations of love and devotion. It was to be 'before the cock crows' that Peter was to crowd in these three occasions of failure. It was not that his faith was worn away by a long process of attrition, or yet that it was shattered by the seeming disaster of crucifixion. Peter fell at the first hurdle, by putting himself in the place of temptation without equipping himself with the armour of truth.

Even if Peter was not ready to follow Jesus to the cross, to follow him into eternity, he could at least have avoided making things worse for Jesus. He could at least have spared Jesus the emotional agony and misery of isolation from his closest friends to add to all the other horrors of Calvary.

Cold comfort

There may be a measure of comfort for us in what happened to Peter. No matter what he did in the short term, the long-term future was secure, because 'his heart was in the right place'. But this is surely cold comfort. for we must realise that every avoidable denial in our lives adds to the suffering of our Lord and Saviour. Prime Minister Margaret Thatcher once commented on a rail disaster, 'Somehow on these distressing occasions we manage to do better than our best.' But on this distressing occasion Peter and the others managed to do worse than their worst.

Peter and the other disciples had to learn that the truth about their humanity was that they were still limited not just by time and space but by fear and spiritual weakness, but that this was not a static frailty but contained the possibility of a growth in strength that would make them of increasing use to the Master and of increasing fitness for Heaven '*afterwards*'.

How often does our productivity fail to match our protestations, what we do having no relation to what we say! One minute Peter is so sure that he would *die* for Jesus. The next minute it becomes evident that he will not only fail to *speak* for Jesus, but that he will vehemently *deny* any knowledge of his Master.

Peter needed to realise his fallibility. His gushing emotion prompted him to promise all. He needed to see himself as Jesus saw him, to see the real, fallible man he was, as yet untransformed, unempowered by the Spirit. Later he might be ready to die for Jesus, but he had a lot of maturing to do before that was true of him.

12. THE TRUTH ABOUT OUR DESTINY

(John 14:1-11)

'There are many rooms in my Father's house, and I am going to prepare a place for you. I would not tell you this if it were not so.' (14:2).

THE wording of the emphatic truth is a little different this time: 'I would not tell you this if it were not so' rather than 'I am telling you the truth', but this verse contains an important truth, so we include it here. There is here a lovely apposition of two contrasting statements, first the bad news, then the good. Jesus has just said: 'You cannot go where I am going' (13:33). But almost immediately he says: 'I am going to prepare a place for you' (14:2). We may not be fit and ready *now*; but we shall be ready *later* if we live by the rule of love, the way of Christ. Ready for what? To go where Jesus has gone. Where is that? To the Father's house.

We may be surprised at his use of the word 'prepare'. What a lot of work there is in us preparing for anything! How many details there are to *think* about in advance, as well as to actually *do*! Yet we might find it rather strange (as Joseph Parker points out) that:

> the divine being, God the Son, should ever have occasion to 'prepare' anything . . . so as to have all things in due proportion and relation, that the eye may be pleased, that the ear may be satisfied, and that all our desires may be met and fulfilled. Why, Jesus Christ talks. . . as if there was a great deal of work for him to do in the way of arranging and ordering and getting things ready for his servants.

Of course, Jesus wasn't without practice in executing important and painstaking work. At the beginning of John's Gospel we are told, 'Through him God made all things; not one thing in all creation was made without him' (1:3).

Celestial overtime

But is there any need for all this celestial overtime, for the Son of God to be burdened with making heavenly beds and preparing a table before us? Surely with his infinite power he could just say the word and it would be done; surely he could create a world or redeem sinful humanity or prepare a place in eternity for us at the snap of a finger, in the twinkling of an eye? But the trouble with that concept is that it could suggest a God who acts at whim, or who doesn't care, who isn't personally involved with man, a God who gets what he wants without effort. We might almost get the idea of a God who 'couldn't care less'. The wonderful thing about the Son of God enduring all the agony of the cross for our redemption and going to endless pains to prepare a place in Heaven for us, is that it makes us realise that in fact God 'couldn't care more'. Jesus is willing to go to all lengths to prepare our way from here to eternity, from here to the hereafter—certainly with infinite power, but also at infinite cost.

Whether to the disciples afraid at the imminent death of their Lord, or to us afraid at the prospect of our own death, this verse comes with wonderful assurance: at greatest cost he is *preparing* a place where we can be in his company. Here is the basic truth about our destiny in eternity.

Questions, questions

But there remains the question of how to get to that prepared place. The disciples are full of questions:

Peter asks:	'Where are you going, Lord?' (13:36);
	'Lord, why can't I follow you now?' (13:37).
Thomas asks:	'Lord, . . . how can we know the way to get there?' (14:5).
Philip asks:	'Lord, show us the Father' (14:8).

Lord, where? Lord, why? Lord, how? Lord, who? They are full of questions, and we might think that Jesus was almost as evasive as a Chancellor of the Exchequer parrying questions before the budget, 'going into purdah' as it is sometimes described. The one answer that Jesus has for the disciples is himself:

'*I am going* to prepare a place for you' (14:2).
'*I will come back* and take you to myself' (14:3).
'*I am* the way, the truth, and the life' (14:6).
'*I am* in the Father and the Father is in me' (14:11).

That one answer 'I am' answers every question.

Thomas says, 'We still don't know where you are going, and we haven't a clue how to get there' (see 14:5), but Jesus tells him that he himself is not just the truth and the life, but he is also the way (14:6).

He is not just the destination but he is also the route. It is the difference between somebody giving you directions—first left, second right, straight on to the roundabout—and you probably get lost before you're halfway there! Or, on the other hand, somebody might say: 'I'm going that way. I'll take you there.' He *becomes* the way.

Philip wants an outside authority to guarantee the process: 'Lord, show us the Father; that is all we need' (14:8). He is saying, in effect, 'Then we will be satisfied!' He wants an introduction to the Father, but Jesus tells him that he himself, the Master whom Philip already knows, is the spitting image of the Father—'If you've seen one, you've seen the other.' There is no need of a guarantor. Christ's word is good enough on its own.

William Barclay writes:

> Jesus is the proof that God is willing to give us everything he has to give. . . . If we believe that in Jesus we see the picture of God, then in face of that amazing love, it becomes, not easy, but at least possible, to accept even what we cannot understand, and in the storms of life to retain a faith that is serene.

So Jesus promises: 'I am going to prepare a place' (14:2). Hebrews 6:20 says, 'On our behalf Jesus has gone in there before us'. In the Greek the word *prodromos* is included. In the Roman army the *prodromoi* were the reconnaissance troops, the vanguard, the trail-blazers. Or another use of the word was of the pilot boat which led ships through difficult and dangerous waters to reach a safe harbour.

Jesus is our *prodromos*. He has gone on ahead but he will come back to welcome us to his ancestral home. He will finish the job. F. W. Boreham writes:

> If any work of God is left unfinished here, it is presumptive, if not conclusive, that he intends to finish it hereafter . . . . Is it conceivable that Almighty God will begin a beautiful painting, and, after a few preliminary touches, toss aside the brushes? Can anybody imagine that, sculptor-like, he will set out to woo an angel from the shapeless marble, and then, tiring of his work, forsake the studio? Would it be like him to write the opening stanzas of one of his sublime poems and then drop the pen, leaving the noble song half-sung? 'I am the Alpha and the Omega', he says, again and again. The meaning is clear. He goes right through. What he commences, he completes. He is the author and the finisher. 'He that hath begun a good work', says Paul, 'will perform it unto the end.' There are no frayed edges or loose ends in the divine handiwork. It follows, therefore, that if, in this life, some divine task is left half-finished, it is because the work will be brought to perfection in some other realm.

So here is the truth about our destiny:

(a)   Heaven is where Jesus is;
(b)   he will come back for us;
(c)   to see Jesus is to see what God is like;
(d)   we will be where he is.

Verily, verily, the truth about our eternal destiny is that Jesus has prepared a place for us. He will complete what he has begun.

Going or coming

There are two more statements that we ought to look at together because they might seem rather contradictory: 'I am *going* to prepare a place for you. . . . I will *come back* and take you to myself' (14:2, 3);

We might ask: 'Is he coming or going?' But precision of definition can be deceiving in spiritual matters. These texts are not so much about physical places as about spiritual states. The truth is a spiritual one, not a geographical one. We must not think in terms of the place where we shall be so much as the person whom we shall be with. It is not so much that we go or that the Father and the Son come, but that we are, or are not, together, completely in spiritual communion. It is a state in which we dwell rather than a place.

But note that the promise is that God the Father is in this with God the Son—'We will come', says Jesus. Dummelow in his commentary says: 'Where the Son is, there of necessity is the Father also, as well as the Spirit, for the Three are One. . . . The persons of the Trinity are inseparable and contain one another.'

So here is another recurring theme. There will be no permanent separation in spite of apparent physical separation:

'I will come back and take you to myself' (14:3).
'I will come back to you. In a little while . . . you will see me' (14:18, 19).
'My Father and I will come to him and live with him' (14:23).
'I am leaving, but I will come back to you' (14:28).

13. THE TRUTH ABOUT OUR CAPABILITY
(John 14:12-14)

'I am telling you the truth: whoever believes in me will do what I do—yes, he will do even greater things, because I am going to the Father' (14:12).

AGAIN we have a pair of staggering statements which at first sight seem somewhat contradictory:

'Whoever believes in me will do what I do—yes, he will do *even greater things*' (14 :12);
'If you ask me for anything in my name, *I* will do it' (14:14).

We can reword them slightly:

You can do greater than *I*;
If *you* ask me, *I* will do anything.

In the first statement there is the *range* of the promise—'Whoever believes in me'. It applies not only to the immediate disciples, but to anyone who believes in Jesus, to us.

Then there is the scope of the promise— 'even greater things' than Jesus himself. What does it mean? Surely we can't believe it because:

(a)   *we* do not achieve dramatic acts of healing;
(b)   *we* do not have crowds following us everywhere;
(c)   *we* seldom say anything very original or of any great value, and our teaching is dependant on *his* teaching.

Greater things

But there are senses in which the statement is quite clearly meaningful:

(a) His earthly achievement was cut short by early death. We spend longer on earth. We have greater opportunity.

(b) He did not commit his teaching to writing, so that at first very few knew about it and we can know of it only at second-hand. Now in

52

our world the ministry of the printed word seems almost to have no end to its scope. We have greater possibilities in communication.

(c) He was seen and heard only by the immediate crowd. If he were ministering in Galilee today, his words could be heard and his face could be seen instantaneously by many nations through television. We have greater opportunities to disseminate the word in preaching.

(d) He was able to feed a relatively small multitude, but today the plight of huge numbers in Ethiopia or Bangladesh or Kurdistan or Armenia may be shown to the world and touch many hearts, so that massive amounts of relief supplies can reach them by air quickly, if governments and others allow that to happen. We have more chance to feed ever greater multitudes.

(e) Jesus was a travelling man, but only in the little land of Palestine. Today a politician's or even a religious leader's travel schedule is almost immeasurably greater. Even our own opportunities for travel are much greater than even half a century ago.

The scope for extension of the Christian gospel, then, is continually multiplied, and even in these difficult days there are more Christians than ever before. In these ways, today's Christians can do 'even greater things', greater even than Jesus or his disciples could do. We sometimes fail to notice this in our amazement at the greater *power* of the acts of Jesus. We may not have the same power, but we have greater *scope*, because of the circumstances of his life, because he lived in ancient times, because he went to his Father at an early age.

And of course in some ways even our powers are greater than those of Jesus:

(a) We talk about 'the miracles of modern medicine'. Barclay says: 'The physician and the surgeon have powers which to the ancient world would have seemed miraculous or even godlike.'

(b) And we talk about 'the miracles of modern science'—for instance, the new genetic fingerprinting technique, by which a criminal's identity can be established from a speck of blood or fluid left behind at the scene of the crime. A genetic profile proved that a Czech spy's 'mother', who had thought for years that he was her long lost son, could not, in fact, be his mother.

So even our powers are in some ways greater than his. But we must balance this. We know that our mental powers are not matched by our moral powers. When it comes to goodness, we still cannot match Jesus.

Spiritual achievement

And we need to balance the statement about 'greater things' with the second verse quoted above, 'If you ask me for anything in my name, I will do it' (v 14):

(a) spiritual achievement comes by prayer;
(b) spiritual achievement comes by prayer for the things which our Lord wants to happen.

In the end spiritual achievement is brought about not by our power, but by God's power. It might look as if we are doing greater things, but it is really the power of God working through us.

So the earthly ministry of Jesus was limited in space and time. The work that the risen Lord will do through those who pray and act 'in his name' is unlimited. Its only limit will be our lack of faith. But it must be done 'in his name', that is, in conformity with his will and purpose. So that all we do is never to our own glory but to the glory of the Father and of the Son: a manifestation of *their* power and *their* love.

There may, however, be a sense in which the 'even greater things' of which Jesus is speaking are not 'of this world' at all. *He* is going to be able to do greater things, *because* he is going to the *Father*. What a happy way to look at death—it is 'going to the Father'. If he had not led the way to the Father, we could not follow. This is a greater thing than any we can accomplish in this life.

Henry Drummond wrote: 'It is not departure, it is arrival; not sleep, but waking. For life to those who live like Christ is not a funeral procession. It is a triumphal march to the Father.'

The same writer comments on the word 'Father':

> Did you ever notice Christ's favourite words? If you have you must have been struck by two things—their simplicity and their fewness. Some half-dozen words embalm all his theology, and these are, without exception, humble, elementary, simple monosyllables. They are such words as these: world, life, trust, love.
>
> But none of these was the greatest word of Christ. His great word was new to religion. There was no word there, when he came, rich enough to carry the new truth he was bringing to men. So he imported into religion one of the grandest words of human language and transfigured it, and gave it back to the world illuminated and transfigured, as the watchword of the new religion. That word was Father.

Just as the final fulfilment of Christ's life and ministry was to be achieved in the hereafter, so we will become our best selves on the other side of death. Jesus teaches us that, if we are his disciples, we go not to a numinous being beyond our comprehension, nor to a fearsome judge, but to a father, to be his children. Yet to be in his presence then, we need to be in his will now.' We must believe in him now and do what he does.

14. THE TRUTH ABOUT OUR COPABILITY
(JOHN 16:4b-15)

'I am telling you the truth: it is better for you that I go away, because if I do not go, the Helper will not come to you. But if I do go away, then I will send him to you' (16:7).

IT is difficult to find a word ending in '-ity' for the title of this chapter, so let's make do with an invented word—*copability*. Are we able to cope with Christ's expectations of us? If we find it difficult to believe:

(a) that we can do greater things than Jesus (14:12);
(b) that what we pray for in his name will happen (14:14);
(c) that we can even 'obey his commandments' (14:15);

then the answer is the *Helper*—the Holy Spirit. By his help we can cope. If we are tempted to say, 'Oh yeah?' to those statements in chapter 14, then we find the answer here in chapter 16. If Jesus seems to take our *capability* for granted, while we have grave doubts about our *copability*, the gap is filled by the Holy Spirit.

The truth is that the disciples will manage much better if Jesus goes away. 'It is better for you that I go away' he tells them, 'because then the Spirit will come.'

Henry Drummond wrote:

> Suppose he had not gone away; suppose he were here now. Suppose he were still in the Holy Land; at Jerusalem. Every ship that started for the east would be crowded with Christian pilgrims. Every train flying through Europe would be thronged with people going to see Jesus. Every mailbag would be full of letters from those in difficulty and trial. Suppose you are in one of those ships. The port, when you arrive after the long voyage, is blocked with vessels of every flag. With much difficulty you land, and join one of the long trains starting for Jerusalem. For as far as the eye can reach, the caravans move over the desert in an endless stream. As you approach the Holy City you see a

dark, seething mass stretching for leagues and leagues between you and its glittering spires. You have come to see Jesus but you will never see him.

How old-fashioned this passage seems! It says nothing about airliners, telephones, fax machines, television, etc. But it is still true. Modern methods of travel would only increase the throng, though the modern media of communication would multiply the number of those who could 'see' him without being 'where he is'. Yet all the potential but unsatisfied pilgrims can have the Helper constantly in their hearts.

The gift of the Spirit

Here then is another of these recurring themes in Jesus' words to his disciples at the Last Supper—the coming of the Holy Spirit; the replacement of the physical presence of the Son by the spiritual presence of the Spirit. Although we are using 16:7 as our main text here, the gift of the Spirit has been a recurring theme from 14:16 onwards. There are in fact five paragraphs about the Spirit in chapters 14 to 16, and in each Jesus makes the same two points.

First, Jesus repeatedly states that the Spirit is sent by the Father and the Son. They are an inseparable trinity of being. They are all in it together. If we know one we know all three! This truth keeps being hammered home:

'Now that you have known me . . . you will know my Father also, and from now on you do know him and you have seen him' (14:7)—if you know the Son, you know the Father.

'You know him [the Spirit], because he remains with you and is in you' (14:17)—if you know the Son, you know the Spirit.

As John Stott says: 'Although each person of the Trinity is eternally distinct from the others . . . yet the three Persons are so completely one in their essential being that to know one is to know the others.'

The second point that Jesus emphasises is that the Spirit has a specific work and that that work is primarily a teaching work.

Now let us look at these twin truths as they recur in chapters 14-16.

14:16-20

The trinitarian formula
'*I* will ask the *Father*, and he will give you another *Helper*' (14:16). If we know one, we know the others.

The Spirit's work
He is the *abiding* Spirit—he 'will stay with you for ever' (14:16); he 'remains with you' (14:17).

56

He is the *indwelling* Spirit—he 'is in you' (14:17).

He is the *revealing* Spirit— he 'reveals the truth about God' to those who know him: 'The world cannot receive him, because it cannot see him or know him' (14:17).

He is the *comforting* Spirit—'You will not be left all alone' (14:18). The Greek word here, *orphanos*, literally means 'orphan', 'without a father'.

14:25-26

The trinitarian formula

'The *Helper*, the *Holy Spirit*, whom the *Father* will send in *my* name' (14:26).

The Spirit's work

He is the *teaching* Spirit—'The Helper . . . will teach you everything and make you remember all that I have told you' (14:25, 26).

Two of the processes of education include:

(a)   getting knowledge into the head of the pupil in the first place;
(b)   getting him to recall it correctly at will.

A tired mind often refuses to produce that piece of information which you know you know but just can't recall. Spiritually speaking, that's the kind of situation in which the Spirit can help us. There is no point in typing data into a word processor, getting it on to the floppy disc if we don't know how to find it again on the disc, and if we don't know how to get a printout.

So the Spirit not only helps us to see the truth and understand it, but he prompts us in making use of it. He helps us to recall the truth when and where it applies in practice. He is a teacher who not only captivates our interest theoretically but helps us practically to apply our knowledge and to pass our tests. He gives us the gift of recalling what he has taught us, the facility of recall.

15:26-27

The trinitarian formula

'The *Helper* will come—the *Spirit* . . . who comes from the *Father*. *I* will send him to you from the *Father*, and he will speak about *me*' (15:26).

The Spirit's work

He is the *revealing* Spirit: he 'reveals the truth about God' (15:26).

He is the *witnessing* Spirit: 'The Helper . . . will speak about me. And you, too, will speak about me' (15:26, 27). We share the Holy Spirit's function of bearing witness to Jesus. But we cannot be a witness without, unless we have the witness within.

16:7-11

The trinitarian formula
'If *I* do not go, the *Helper* will not come to you. But if *I* do go away, then *I* will send *him* to you' (16:7). (The Father is not specifically mentioned this time but his involvement may be understood from foregoing passages.)

The Spirit's work
He is the *reproving* Spirit—'When he comes, he will prove to the people of the world that they are wrong about sin and about what is right and about God's judgement' (16:8).

Again, there seems rather a contradiction when we read this in apposition to 14:17: 'The world cannot receive him, because it cannot see him or know him.' But note that this verse is talking about receiving him while the above passage is telling of his witness to men. The fact that the world chooses to pay no notice to what the Spirit is saying to it does not mean that he ceases to speak to it. He is constantly reproving, convicting, convincing—in so far as the world will listen. There is a relationship with the Spirit that Christians alone can know but that does not mean that he ceases to speak to those who have not received him.

16:13-15

The trinitarian formula
'*He* will take what *I* say and tell it to you. All that *my Father* has is mine; that is why *I* said that the *Spirit* will take what *I* give *him* and tell it to you' (16:14, 15).

The Spirit's work
He is the *revealing* Spirit—he 'reveals the truth about God, he will lead you into all the truth' (16:13).
He is the *prophesying* Spirit—'He will not speak on his own authority, but he will speak of what he hears, and will tell you of things to come' (16:13). But his prophesying will be an evolution of what Jesus has already taught. There will be continuity. His disciples needn't be afraid that they will be led astray. The 'all the truth' that the Spirit will bring, the whole truth, will simply be an amplification of the truth that they know now in the one who has just said, 'I am the way, the truth, and the life' (14:6). As one writer has put it: 'They are not ready yet to grasp the full meaning of their master's words, of his oncoming death. Only after the Resurrection will

their eyes open. Only when the Spirit is shed upon them will they be ready for a public proclamation of their faith.'

He is the *glorifying* Spirit—'He will give me glory' (16:14).

He is the *go-between* Spirit—'He will take what I say and tell it to you' (16:14); 'The Spirit will take what I give him and tell it to you' (16:15).

Our copability is greatly enhanced by the presence of the Helper.

15. THE TRUTH ABOUT OUR VULNERABILITY
(John 16:16-22)

'I am telling you the truth: you will cry and weep, but the world will be glad; you will be sad, but your sadness will turn into gladness . . . . the kind of gladness that no one can take away from you' (16:20, 22).

THIS passage begins with confusion over the phrases 'in a little while' and 'a little while later' (see Key 7 for further discussion on the use of such phrases in John's Gospel). The disciples are confused (16:17, 18) and Jesus knows it (16:19). One clue to the meaning of these phrases is that the disciples quote Jesus as saying (16:17): 'It is because I am going to the Father' (see 16:10). So the 'little while' is linked to Jesus leaving the world, and therefore the first 'little while' may well mean the time between the crucifixion and the Resurrection, and the second 'little while' would then mean the post-Resurrection period when they would see Jesus again.

The day of the Lord

On the other hand, Jesus *could* possibly be referring to his second coming, the full coming of his Kingdom, as has sometimes been assumed. The picture of the woman in labour was used in the Old Testament to describe 'the day of the Lord', a terrible time between the present age and the age to come. Before the golden age of God came, there would be a time in which the present world would be shattered to fragments, as this extract from Isaiah 13:6-10 illustrates:

> The day of the Lord is near, the day when the Almighty brings destruction. . . . They will all be terrified and overcome with pain, like the pain of a woman in labour. They will look at each other in fear, and their faces will burn with shame. The day of the Lord is coming—that cruel day of his fierce anger and fury. The earth will be made a wilderness, and every sinner will be destroyed.

So it would be possible to conclude that Jesus is speaking by allusion of the birth-pangs of the full coming of his Kingdom, and that where he talks of 'that day' he is in fact talking of 'the day of the Lord', though that is not the obvious meaning.

Whatever the context, Jesus is saying that his people will have to go through terrible things but if they endure to the end it will all be worth while.

There will be a role reversal between the world and the Christian. The Christian's sorrow will turn to joy. The world's careless joy will turn to sorrow. There is an inverse ratio between the world's sadness and gladness and ours. When the world is top dog, we may well be having a hard time, for the world's perception of what gives satisfaction is upside down. But there are two compensating factors in the Christian's reaction to sadness.

Redeemed sadness

First, the Christian has the ability to redeem his sadness. Leslie Weatherhead tells how he asked a man, 'Why does your wife never come with you to church?' 'Well,' he replied, 'On the night our boy was killed in France in the war she stopped praying. She has never had anything to do with God since.' Weatherhead describes her as tight-lipped, cynical, bitter. No one cared for her very much. No one loved her very dearly, because she found it impossible to love anybody else. Her brain was like lead and her heart like ice, all because of her attitude to sorrow.

In contrast, think of a story told by Dr Stanley Jones:

> In Fuchow there are three graves side by side. Two of them were the graves of the daughters of a widow in Australia. Those two girls went out as missionaries to China and they were both murdered. When the news came to the widow in Australia that her daughters had been killed, she was sixty-two years of age. . . . She sold all that she had. She went to the place where her two girls had been murdered. She learnt the Chinese language, set up a school, and gave twenty years of service to China. She died at the age of eighty-two and was buried near her daughters.

Obviously neither woman welcomed the pain of her bereavement, but one bore it negatively, while the other responded positively and redeemed her sorrow, to the blessing of herself and others. 'You will be sad, but your sadness will turn to gladness,' promises Jesus.

Pain with a purpose

The second compensating factor is that the Christian's sadness is temporary. It is pain with a purpose. It has a future in it, like the

61

tribulations of a woman in labour, which are changed to the joys of motherhood. The joys of motherhood cannot be experienced without the pain of labour: 'When a woman is about to give birth, she is sad because her hour of suffering has come; but when the baby is born, she forgets her suffering, because she is happy that a baby is born into the world' (16:21).

The pain will be forgotten. The remarkable thing about labour pains seems to be that mothers almost immediately forget them. They do not hold them against the child, or against the husband or against God. That time of pain does not stop them from conceiving other children. The pain is soon forgotten in the joy of the new life. Floyd Filson writes: 'After the short period of birth pains her anguish is past, her sorrow forgotten, and she rejoices in possessing the child that has been born.'

Similarly the tribulations of a Christian are bearable because they lead to the new life of eternity, and that kind of gladness is something that cannot be taken away (16:22).

What, then, is the joy that no one can take away? David Guthrie has said:

> The deepest joy comes from that which we value the most. When we centre our lives on our relationship with God . . . we have something that can never be lost, and is always, whatever our circumstances, present. No person can rob us, the state can't legislate it away, not even our death can intervene. Nothing can separate us from the love of God. . . . Everything else—but everything—will be lost to us: home, spouse, children, health— finally life itself. The only value that remains is God. . . . Everyone—at least potentially—derives joy from what they value and especially from what they centrally value. What distinguishes the Christian is that the joy in God is unclouded by the prospect that it must all come to an end.

Our vulnerability is made bearable by our immortality.

16. THE TRUTH ABOUT OUR SUFFICIENCY
(John 16:23-28)

'When that day comes, you will not ask me for anything. I am telling you the truth: the Father will give you whatever you ask him for in my name' (16:23).

'When that day comes, you will ask him in my name; and I do not say that I will ask him on your behalf, for the Father himself loves you' (16:26, 27).

THE stated truth here about our sufficiency is that we get what we ask for, *if it is in accordance with God's will.* It is interesting to note that there are two different Greek words here which are translated 'ask':

(a) 'You will not *ask me* for anything'—this is the Greek verb *erotao*—more often used of 'asking a question', asking for an answer, so a better translation might be 'You will no longer ask me anything' (as in the *NIV*);

(b) 'The Father will give you whatever you *ask* him for'—here the word is *aiteo*—which usually refers to asking *for* something.

We may make this same distinction when we say, 'I asked him something' and 'I asked him for something' or when we say, 'I questioned him' and 'I requested something'.
(There is, however, some degree of overlap in the meaning of the two words, but the use of both in the same verse does suggest an intentional distinction.)

Questions answered, needs supplied

Jesus is really making two promises. First, he tells them that they will not need to ask any more questions. They will '*know* it all.' There will be fullness of *knowledge*. In the Gospels in general, and in these chapters that we are studying in particular, the disciples were *always* asking questions. Now Jesus is not saying to them: 'You *must* not ask me any questions' but 'You *will* not ask me any questions. There will be no need. It will all be crystal clear.' They will enjoy what R. M. Benson calls 'the perfect illumination of grace'.

Then, secondly, Jesus says that not only will all their questions be answered, but their *needs* will all be supplied. They will *have* it all! Now this is not to say that prayer is a slot-machine. We don't just press the button and get what we ask for. As Reginald Hollis says:

> Magic prayer would bring out the worst in us. Aunt Meg who was leaving a large fortune would be prayed to death by those who expected to inherit it. Grandma would be kept alive by prayer as long as she was a useful free babysitter and didn't interfere. If we could do everything by magic prayer, most of us would give up working. We would be flabby, spoiled, selfish children. That kind of thinking about prayer is not what Jesus had to say about prayer.

There are three limitations on the promise in the context. The first is 'whatever you ask him for'. James Martin says:

> The trouble is lack of ambition. We are quite content with what Jesus Christ has already done for us and have no real desire that he should do anything more. It is enough for us that we have crossed the border into his Kingdom of life. We have no yearning to explore it further and to possess it more fully.

Secondly, Jesus says 'when that day comes' (16:26). 'That day' is often taken to mean the full coming of the Kingdom, but if we read the saying in context, it appears to refer to the time of sadness, suffering and persecution foreseen in 16:20-22. The promise is for this 'vale of tears'.

In my name

A third limitation is 'in my name' (see also 14:13, 14 and 15:16). William Temple says that 'the essential act of prayer is not the bending of God's will to ours—of course not—but the bending of our will to his.' It is not that when we say 'in Jesus' name' we automatically get what we ask for. It is rather that when what we ask for is truly according to the nature and purpose of Jesus (and therefore of God the Father) then it will be granted. In one sense this puts a limit on what we ask. Our requests must be such that Jesus would approve them. Reginald Hollis has also written:

> Some people might think it presumptuous to think we could know the Lord's will, but surely that is why Jesus lived. If we study . . . the record of his life, there are many things that are indisputably God's will. We know, for instance, that his will is the healing of disease, since Jesus spent much time . . . healing those who were sick. . . . We know that Jesus' will is the spread

of his truth, for he told his disciples to go into all the world and preach the gospel.

On the other hand, there may well be other things that we know quite certainly that we should not pray for, because we know that they are not in God's will. 'In Jesus' name' limits what we ask.

In another sense, the fact that we must pray in Jesus' name opens up many more possibilities to us. If we were handling the finances of a firm we might be able to go to a bank and cash a cheque for a huge amount of money. We would do it *in the name of the firm* and there would be no question. But if we went into the same bank with a cheque for the same amount, but *in our own name*, we would probably get nothing. So if we present our requests in the name and for the sake of Jesus, there is always a credit balance and the Father will pay out. Prayer broadens our horizons and enhances our abilities.

We must note also the statement in 16:24: 'Until now you have not asked for anything.' Taken in context, this is not a comment on the disciples' prayerlessness (or ours). It refers rather to the establishment of a new kind of prayer—Christian prayer. Up till now the disciples had presumably been praying the formalised prayers of devout Judaism (no doubt with the addition of the Lord's Prayer). From our standpoint of prolonged Christian tradition, it is perhaps difficult for us to appreciate the revolutionary nature of the new spiritual provision Jesus is making for his disciples on this last night—prayer in his name that will guarantee an answer, and the gift of the Spirit as the one who stands by them.

However, most of us will have to admit that it is the sad truth that we have not asked much in Jesus' name. We haven't been very adventurous in our *requests*, so we have not been very receptive of his *bequests*. We have not sought as we ought. We have not believed, so we have not received.

> We have not served thee as we ought;
>   Alas the duties left undone,
> The work with little fervour wrought,
>   The battles lost or scarcely won!
> Lord, give the zeal, and give the might,
>   For thee to toil, for thee to fight.

(Thomas Benson Pollock,
The song book of The Salvation Army, No 466)

But even if we have asked, we have not always received. Doubtless this is often because we have not asked 'in his name'. But are there not also many other occasions when we are forced to ask 'Why doesn't God do something about it?'—occasions when we simply do not have enough knowledge about God's will and about the ultimate consequences of the events of which we are a part.

A greater purpose

In the classic Old Testament story of Job, we may overlook the fact that there was a greater purpose *of which he was unaware*. He was afflicted to the point of total disaster—the loss of his not-inconsiderable assets, the destruction of his lovely children, the damaged health of his own body. His friends plagued him with 'good' but insensitive advice, assuming that his fate was due to his fault—in itself a hard thing to bear. How can God allow a good man like him to suffer so? Yet for all his disasters and doubts Job still said in the end: 'Though he [God] slay me, yet will I trust in him' (13:15, *AV*).

Remember, too, that while Job was thus keeping faith, he was *unknowingly* part of a greater purpose. The first two chapters of Job show us that he was part of the great struggle between good and evil, between God and Satan. This is graphically illustrated by the story of a conversation between God and Satan. God uses Job as an example of a man who is good and faithful, untouched by evil. Satan retorts, 'Only because you look after him; because nothing unpleasant ever happens to him.' So God allows Job to suffer to show that he is a man who is truly good, and not just because of what he can get out of it.

But Job has no knowledge of this heavenly dialogue. He is in the dark about the heroic part he is called to play in this struggle. Yet he still doggedly maintains his goodness and his faith. Perhaps part of the truth about our suffering is that we are being given an opportunity to prove, in far less dramatic ways perhaps, that our love for God has nothing to do with our well-being. We might not be able to see it at the time, but might it not have something to do with God's struggle against spiritual evil?

And if we want our ignorance and our mystification put into perspective, we need to read the closing chapters of Job (38-42), with his final response to God:

> I talked about things I did not understand . . .
>   but now I have seen you with my own eyes.
> So I am ashamed of all I have said
>   and repent in dust and ashes.

> (42:3-6).

Often we may still not understand but we press on in hope and faith, believing that in the wisdom of God our suffering makes sense. 'In my name' is no magic formula for getting what we want, but an opportunity to co-operate, sometimes without having a clue how, in getting what God wants!

17. THE TRUTH ABOUT OUR MATURITY
(John 21:15-19)

'I am telling you the truth: when you were young, you used to get ready and go anywhere you wanted to; but when you are old, you will stretch out your hands and someone else will bind you and take you where you don't want to go. . . . Follow me!' (21:18, 19).

THE final occasion in John's Gospel where we find our key phrase— 'I am telling you the truth'—is very near the end. We should first note that this saying is personally addressed to Peter. When last a 'verily, verily' statement was addressed to him it was a prediction of his denials (13:38). Now he has been led by the risen Christ through a question-and-answer session designed to cancel out that threefold denial on the eve of Jesus' crucifixion. Just as he had denied Jesus three times, he is given three opportunities to reaffirm his love for Jesus, together with a three-fold statement of his task in the establishment and care of the infant Church.

We must remember that Peter had been given this task when he made his great confession at Caesarea Philippi: 'You are the Messiah, the Son of the living God' (Matthew 16:16). Jesus told him then, 'Peter: you are a rock, and on this rock foundation I will build my church' (Matthew 16:18). But he had thrown away this privilege by his denials and Jesus now makes this point subtly by addressing him by his old name, Simon, and he makes him aware that he is on trial and that his remarks are crucial by using his *full* name, 'Simon son of John'. So he is back where he was at the time of his first call, and each of his denials must be cancelled out before his relationship with Jesus and his position in the Church can be re-established.

Love—or 'love'

It is interesting to note that two different Greek words are used for the verb 'love', with a significance that is not always captured in translation. The first is *agapao*, which is used nearly always of the love of God to us or of our love for him and our fellows— a pure, self-

67

sacrificing love. On the other hand *phileo* is the ordinary word used of close friendship. So when Jesus asks his three questions he begins by using *agapao*: 'Do you love me with a self-renouncing love and do you love me more than these others?' Peter finds he cannot claim either an *agape* love, or a greater love than others. He can only claim a *philia* love—the love of a close friend.

Jesus' second question scales down the demand: 'Never mind about other people, then, do you love me with a self-renouncing love?' (*agape*)? Again Peter, conscious of his previous failing, can only suggest his unworthiness, by claiming only a friend's love (*philia*).

Then again Jesus reduces his demands, and asks only if Peter genuinely has a friend's deep love. At this Peter gets rather hot-under-the-collar as we all tend to do when being cross-examined, and especially when we know we are in the wrong. He really had no right to be annoyed, of course. He was being given the opportunity to cancel out his sin, an opportunity that others do not always share. We may be forgiven, but we do not always have the opportunity to put things right.

So Jesus' questioning becomes less and less demanding until he arrives at a statement that Peter can accept: 'Do you love me as a true friend?' This is a position from which Jesus can begin to build Peter up again into the rock of faith he needs for the foundation of his Church.

We may note too that the three commands given to Peter also vary somewhat in the words used. Literally translated, they read: 'Feed my little lambs'; 'Shepherd my little sheep'; 'Feed my little sheep'. There are two tasks involved—to 'feed' and to 'shepherd'. The modern equivalent of these two tasks for those who follow Peter in ministry might well be to preach and to pastor. In each of the three references to the flock, the words used each have a diminutive element in their meaning, suggesting affection. We might almost translate, 'my dear little lambs'.

In Peter's first call (Luke 5:1-11) the fishermen had been asked to 'catch men'. Now in his re-call the fisherman is to become a shepherd, a reminder that evangelism is not the whole of the Christian ministry. Shepherding is equally important.

Peter's fate

It is not certain to whom the 'truth' in 21:18 is addressed. Is the 'you' singular (ie addressed to Peter) or plural (for general application)? That it was primarily a particular word for Peter is suggested in verse 19, where it seems to be an indication of Peter's future fate: '*You* will stretch out your hands and someone else will bind you and take you where you don't want to go.'

William Temple in his *Readings in St John's Gospel* says that, as the words of Jesus stand, they suggest only that Peter will have his future taken out of his hands:

> Once Peter had been wilful and headstrong. . . . He chose his own path and walked where he would. As the ardour of youth cools and the feebleness of age comes on, all this will change. He will stretch forth his hands as he gropes along unknown ways, and others will carry him against his choice.

However, John in retrospect makes his own comment, which suggests a more specific meaning for the saying relating to martyrdom: 'In saying this, Jesus was indicating the way in which Peter would die and bring glory to God' (21:19). A few days earlier, the Lord had said, 'You cannot go where I am going' (13:33), but now he says to Peter 'Follow me!' (21:19). In the power of the Spirit it is becoming possible for Peter to follow Jesus 'even unto death'.

Glorious passivity

Perhaps, however, we may also look at this final 'truth' in 21:18 in a more general way as a comment on the impulsiveness and vigorous self-fulfilment of youth, and, in contrast, the self-abnegation of old age. Is this not a valid picture of the development of spiritual maturity? The young Christian may draw attention by his vigour, determination and direction, but the characteristic of the mature disciple may be (as Temple again suggests) not so much what he does, but what he allows to be done to him: 'His passivity is more powerful than his acts.' Jesus' 'glory' is not in lifting himself up but in his being lifted up. He reigns from a gallows. Peter will have to learn that it is not in self-aggrandisement or in self-protection, but in self-giving or even self-losing, that true spiritual greatness lies.

Robert Llewelyn (in *With pity not with blame*) also sees this saying as indicating a progression in humility:

> The distinction [is] that in the first case I initiate events and remain in control, whereas in the second something is done to me outside my control, evoking from me one or another type of response.

The difference is between disciplining oneself and patiently accepting discipline from an outside source. Llewelyn adds:

> Once we have shown ourselves ready to enter the shallows, it will not be long before God summons us into deeper waters.

So we too must learn the lesson. There is a time and a place for zest and drive and innovation, but the point at which the tyre of faith really bites the road of service is the point of suffering and self-sacrifice—when the motionless body can do little but hang from the nails of hostility, while the marred visage can do no more than beam out the evidence of sacrificial love. The triumph of Christ is that it is at the lowest point of physical existence that the majesty and glory of God's mercy and God's love is best seen. 'The cross stands for the best that men can do as well as the worst '(Frederick Buechner).

This is the truth about spiritual maturity.

KEY 6

THE PURPOSE OF THE TRUTH

THERE is yet another set of verses interwoven with these great truths which have been opening up to us by the use of Key 5. Jesus keeps on telling the disciples *why* he is telling them these truths. He wants them to be quite clear why he is talking to them like this. As he lays out these great truths before them on his last night with them, he often tells them 'This is why', introducing his reasons by saying, 'I am telling you . . . *so that . . .*'.

1. First, then, Jesus tells the disciples these truths as *a basis for future trust*:

> 'I tell you this now before it happens, *so that* when it does happen, you will believe that "I Am Who I Am" ' (13:19).

Or as J. B. Phillips translates it: 'From now onwards, I shall tell you things before they happen, *so that* when they do happen, you may believe I am the One I claim to be.'

This verse comes shortly *after* the washing of the disciples' feet and the outlining of the first great truth about humility and responsibility, and it comes immediately *after* Jesus identified his betrayer with the words, 'The man who shared my food turned against me' (13:18). And it *preceeds* the great truth about loyalty and betrayal: 'One of you is going to betray me' (13:21).

So Jesus is in fact saying, 'I'm telling you the truth *so that*, although I'm acting as a servant to you and am going to be betrayed by one of you, you may still believe in me, you will believe that "*I Am Who I Am*".' Remember that these are the very words used by God to identify himself to Moses. So Jesus is saying, 'It certainly isn't going to look like I am God, but I am, and I am telling you in advance about the betrayal, as a basis of future trust.'

2. Jesus tells them the truth as *a basis for future understanding*:

> 'I have told you this while I am still with you. The Helper, the Holy Spirit, whom the Father will send in my name, will teach

71

you everything and make you remember all that I have told you' (14:25).

Judas, not Judas Iscariot but the other disciple of that name, asks the question: 'How can it be that you will reveal yourself to us and not to the world?' (14:22). Jesus says that those who love him will obey his teaching which comes from the Father (14:24); and that they (and only they) will be able to understand his teaching because the Helper will teach them everything and enable them remember it all (14:26). So Jesus is telling them about the Helper, as *a basis for future understanding—so that* they will know what Jesus wants, when he has gone.

3. The truth will also be *a basis for future faith*:

'I have told you this now before it all happens, *so that* when it does happen, you will believe' (14:29).

He has told the disciples he is going away, though he has promised them peace. In a minute (14:30) it becomes evident that the authorities are nearby and they have to move—'Come, let us go from this place' (14:31)—from the Upper Room through the Temple Courts (the reference to the real vine in chapter 15 may have been suggested by the vine carved over the entrance to the Temple) and towards Gethsemane. They are at panic stations! They need *a basis for future faith*, so he hurriedly tells them, 'Do not be worried and upset; do not be afraid' (14:27). 'Remember, I'm coming back! You're not being totally abandoned. Just hang in there and it will all work out!'

4. These truths will also be *a basis for future joy*:

'I have told you this *so that* my joy may be in you and that your joy may be complete' (15:11).

This is perhaps the most surprising result of all. It is just sandwiched in here in a single verse after the teaching on the vine. They are to share his *joy*. Joy of all things! In these circumstances! They might even have been skulking in the Garden of Gethsemane by now. He has told them of betrayal, of denial, of farewell, of death, of going to the Father, and now he expects them to be joyful!

But yes, that is why he is telling them the truth about so many things, *so that* they won't be drowned in despair, *so that* they will still realise the possibility of a future, because they will see that, in spite of the terrible prospect he is facing up to, he still has a deep joy in his heart. 'The joy of unbroken communion with the Father; the joy of a world redeemed by him from selfishness and mutual destruction to love and abundant life; the "joy that was set before him" (Hebrews 12:2, *AV*). The disciples could have joy of that same substance and quality' (William Temple).

5. Truth will also be *a basis of future stability in the faith*:

> 'I have told you this, *so that* you will not give up your faith' (16:1).

Jesus has been talking about the Helper again. He wants them to realise that they are going to have help, the help of the Holy Spirit, as a basis for future stability. And they're certainly going to need it if they are going to hang on to their faith. All the trappings of their religion are going to be denied them. Verse 2 foresees them being thrown out of the synagogues, excommunicated from the faith of their fathers. (See John 12:42, 43 in the Phillips translation: 'Many even of the authorities did believe in him. But they did not admit it for fear of the Pharisees, in case they should be excommunicated.') And 16:2 says also that they'll have a price on their heads and anybody who kills them will think he is a saint for doing so. All their visible means of religious support will disappear, but they will be able to survive if they hang on to the help of the Holy Spirit. That will be the basis of their future stability.

6. Knowing the truth will also be *the basis of their future strength*:

> 'I have told you this, *so that* when the time comes for them to do these things [persecution], you will remember that I told you' (16:4).

'Remember what I've told you!' says a mother when her child goes out into the world to face its dangers, and she hopes that the remembrance will be a strength in face of those dangers. So Jesus says to the Twelve: 'I'm telling you a lot of things to remember *so that*, when the "slings and arrows" assault you, you can be strong.'

7. What he has told them will be *the basis of their future learning*:

> 'I have much more to tell you, but now it would be too much for you to bear' (16:12).

Jesus has told them many things *so that* they might be equipped to survive the days ahead. But he hasn't told them everything. There are more lessons and deeper truths yet to be absorbed. Probably he couldn't tell them everything because some of his lessons could only be understood when they had experienced Calvary and the Resurrection, the Forty Days, followed by the Ascension and Pentecost. You can't understand algebra until you can multiply two by two. There were many lessons still to learn, but now they had *the basis for future learning*.

8. The final reason that Jesus gives for this intensive indoctrination in his few final frantic hours is that it will be *a basis for future security*:

> 'I have told you this *so that* you will have peace by being united to me' (16:33).

The time is coming when they will be physically separated, skulking in their own homes, and Jesus will be left alone—but not really alone because the Father is with him. And just as Jesus and the Father are united, so the disciples can still be united with him, though physically separated, though separated even by death (16:32). He will suffer, they will suffer, but they will be united (16:33). *They* can be brave because *he* has overcome the world. Perhaps he wants their moral support, but they will certainly need his, and because they understand now the basics of what is happening, what it's all about, they will begin to work out the meaning of their future discipleship, on which foundation the Church will be built.

So the great aim of the great Teacher in this great farewell meeting is to leave his learners with a core of great truths, which will be the basis of their future development—a basis for future trust, future understanding, future faith, future joy, future stability, future strength, future learning and future security. We, too, can experience such a future.

KEY 7

WATCHING THE CLOCK

1. NOW IS THE HOUR

A FINAL key to the understanding of John's Gospel may be found in a study of the use of words and phrases concerning time and eternity, like 'the time', 'the hour', 'the day' etc. There is in the fourth Gospel a distinctive emphasis on what is called 'realised eschatology' or 'inaugurated eschatology'. Eschatology is the study of 'last things'— what Stephen Smalley describes as 'what is to happen to the world and especially to man at the end of all things', but realised eschatology suggests that the Kingdom has already come.

There are a few passages in the fourth Gospel which sound out the note of consummation, the gathering up of all things at the end of time. But even when John is using such sayings, he usually balances them with a statement which shows that the good things of the Kingdom of God are not all in the future, but have, at least in part, been realised already in the life of believers. For example:

'*The time is coming* when all the dead will hear his voice and come out of their graves: those who have done good will rise and live, and those who have done evil will rise and be condemned' (5:28, 29)—but:

'Whoever hears my words and believes in him who sent me *has* eternal life. He will not be judged, but *has already* passed from death to life' (5:24).

Again:

'I will raise them to life *on the last day* (6:40)—but:

'He who believes *has* eternal life' (6:47).

Verses 39, 40, 44, 54 of chapter 6 all use the words '*on the last day*'. So it is the Father's will that believers will be raised '*on the last day*'. But in the midst of the passage there is a statement (6:47) which suggests that in a sense by their faith they already possess that eternal life. It is a foregone conclusion.

75

The illustrated Bible dictionary says:

> The distinctive character of New Testament eschatology is determined by the conviction that in the history of Jesus Christ God's decisive eschatological act has already taken place, though in such a way that the consummation remains still future. There is in New Testament eschatology an 'already' of accomplished fulfilment and a 'not yet' of still outstanding promise. There is both a 'realised' and a 'future' aspect.

A time that is coming

On three occasions John uses a special verbal formula—'the time is coming . . . the time has already come'—which seems almost contradictory at first sight, but which graphically displays the fact that our destiny is both realised in the present and fulfilled in 'the time that is coming' (though that may mean different things in different cases). On each of the three occasions the Greek word translated 'time' is in fact the more exact word for 'hour' (*hora*):

'But the time *is coming* and *is already here*, when by the power of God's Spirit people will worship the Father as he really is, offering him the true worship that he wants' (4:23).

'The time *is coming*—the time *has already come*—when the dead will hear the voice of the Son of God, and those who hear it will come to life' (5:25).

'The time *is coming*, and *is already here*, when all of you will be scattered, each one to his own home, and I will be left all alone' (l6:32).

It could be that in these three verses Jesus is talking of a time which has been foretold by Old Testament prophets as 'coming', but which has in fact arrived in Jesus. It may be that the above verses refer back to the words of the prophets:

> 4:23 could refer to Zephaniah 2:11: 'Every nation will worship him, each in its own land.'
> 5:25 reminds us of Isaiah 26:l9: 'Those of our people who have died will live again!'
> 16:32 may echo Zechariah 13:7: 'The Lord Almighty says, "Wake up, sword. and attack the shepherd who works for me! Kill him, and the sheep will be scattered." ' Certainly this text was in Jesus' mind at this time (Mark 14:27) and was soon fulfilled (Mark 14:50).

It is interesting to note that elsewhere in John's Gospel the word 'hour' (*hora*) is used to designate a particular significant period in Jesus' life. When in the original Greek it is preceded by 'an'—the indefinite article (4:21, 23; 5:25, 28, 29; 16:2, 25, 32)—it refers to a time not yet come, ie after the Resurrection. In other instances it is used with a definite article or possessive article—'my' (2:4); 'his' (7:30; 8:20); 'the' (12:23; 13:1; 17:1) and 'this' (12:27). In these cases it refers to the specific season of Christ's return to the Father (13:1), the time when Jesus' destiny will be fulfilled, the period stretching from Palm Sunday to Easter Sunday. 'Now is the hour' for which he was born. (The distinction between these usages is clear in the *NIV*.)

If we move on to another Greek word for a specific time (*hemer*—'day'), we shall find it used only three times, each time with the demonstrative adjective 'that' or 'yonder' (*ekeinos*), 'when that day comes', referring to that which is 'distant' or 'great' (14:20; 16:23, 26). But in none of these cases does the context necessarily suggest the time of 'the end of all things' but rather a state of affairs after the resurrection of Christ and the gift of the Spirit.

Realised eschatology

So we conclude that though there are few references in John to a distant time of completion of God's plan for mankind, there is in his Gospel an emphasis on 'realised eschatology'—an intriguing double perspective or dual polarity in the teaching of Jesus. He comes *now* and he will also *come again*. Salvation is a possibility for the believer in the *present*, and also in the *future*. John emphasises that the coming of the Kingdom of God is a *present* as well as a *future* reality: '*Now* is the time for this world to be judged; *now* the ruler of this world will be overthrown' (12:31).

As Stephen Smalley puts it: 'Christ makes eternal life available in time as well as eternity, and the believer is able by faith to share it at any moment.'

And Dr George R. Beasley-Murray says:

> The Evangelist [John] consistently represents the new existence in Christ by the Spirit to be a *present* reality. Life in the Kingdom of God or new creation is *now*, not a hope reserved for the future. . . . Through Christ the new age of life eternal has come and the new creation is here.

2. WHAT TIME IS IT?

AS we have already noted, chapters 13 to 16, at which we have been looking in detail, are especially rich in words and phrases expressing concepts of time: 'a little while', 'when that time comes', 'I have told you . . . so that', 'now . . . later', 'I will come back', etc. They are closely interwoven and the tendency has been to look at these verses in terms of the 'end of all things', whether that was to be soon, or a very long time away. But there is no need to interpret many of these sayings in that way. In fact it often requires some mental gymnastics to do so. So that when Jesus keeps saying 'in a little while', it is sometimes assumed that we should not take him literally, but rather believe that he was referring to what has turned out to be a very long time, ie the second coming. This requires us to conclude that he was mistaken as to its timing. It is much simpler, and less derogatory to Jesus' understanding, to accept that he did mean 'a little while', ie sometime in the fairly near future, so that he says relatively little about 'last things' as such, and is more interested in the vital inter-relation between time and eternity. Jesus' great concern in these hours when he has a final teaching session with his disciples is for the future development of their spiritual experience, and his focus is relatively short-term.

So there is little that needs to be read in the context of the second coming. It is only in retrospect, knowing how important eternity became to persecuted Christians later, that we would think of interpreting most of these statements in terms of distant 'last things'.

Now . . . and later

Let us, therefore, look at possible interpretations of these sayings of Jesus in the time scale of crucifixion, Resurrection, Ascension, and the coming of the Spirit. (In the following verses, common verbal key words found in these chapters are italicised.) We shall allocate the sayings of Jesus as they appear to relate to the various stages mentioned above.

1. The present crucifixion crisis ('now' or similar expressions of present time). That time will be:

(a) *A time of puzzlement for the disciples*
'You do not understand *now* what I am doing, but you will understand *later*' (13 :7).
'I tell you this *now* before it happens, so that *when it does happen*, you will believe . . .' (13:19—this refers to the betrayal by Judas).
'I have much more to tell you, but *now* it would be too much for you to bear' (16:12).

(b) *A time of glorification for the Son of Man*
'*Now* the Son of Man's glory is revealed; *now* God's glory is revealed through him (13:31).
'Father, *the hour has come*. Give glory to your Son, so that the Son may give glory to you (17:1).

(c) *A time of separation*
'I tell you *now*. . . . You cannot go where I am going' (13:33).
'I did not tell you these things at the beginning. . . . And *now* that I have told you, your hearts are full of sadness. But I am telling you the truth: it is better for you that I go away' (16:4, 6, 7).
'Do you believe *now*? The time is coming, and is already here, when all of you will be scattered, each one to his own home, and I will be left all alone' (16:31, 32).

(d) *A time of fuller knowledge of the Father*
'*Now* that you have known me . . . you will know my Father also, and *from now on* you do know him and you have seen him' (14:7).

(e) *A time of joy and peace*
'I have told you this *so that* my joy may be in you and that your joy may be complete' (15:11).
'I have told you this *so that* you will have peace by being united to me' (16:33).

2. The time of Jesus' Resurrection
Now you see me; now you don't; now you see me again! That is what Jesus is telling the disciples.
'When I go, you will not be left all alone; I will come back to you. In a little while the world will see me no more, but you will see me; and because I live, you also will live' (14:18, 19).
'You heard me say to you, "I am leaving, but I will come back to you." If you loved me, you would be glad that I am going to the Father;

for he is greater than I. I have told you this now before it all happens, so that when it does happen, you will believe' (14:28, 29).

'In a while you will not see me any more, and then a little while later you will see me' (16:16; see also in 16:17-19). 'Your sadness will turn into gladness' (16:20).

'*Now* you are sad, but I will see you again, and your hearts will be filled with gladness, the kind of gladness that no one can take away from you' (16:22).

3. The coming of the Spirit

There are several passages in chapters 14 to 16 which directly foretell the coming of the Spirit (14:16, 17; 14:25, 26; 15:26, 27; 16:4b-15) and we must read other associated sentences in that context. For example:

'*When that day comes*, you will know that I am in my Father and that you are in me, just as I am in you. . . . Whoever loves me will obey my teaching. . . . My Father and I will come to him and live with him' (14:20, 23).

'I have told you this *while I am still with you*. The Helper . . . will teach you everything and make you remember all that I have told you' (14:25, 26).

'I have much more to tell you, but now it would be too much for you to bear. *When, however, the Spirit comes* . . . he will lead you into all truth' (16:12, 13).

4. The post-Pentecost era

'You cannot follow me *now* where I am going . . . but *later* you will follow me' (13:36). As we have seen, this may have been a word spoken specifically to Peter who boasts that he is ready for martyrdom, so this sentence perhaps refers to Peter's crucifixion, rather than being a general statement.

'You will be expelled from the synagogues, and *the time will come* when anyone who kills you will think that by doing this he is serving God. . . . *When the time comes* for them to do these things, you will remember that I told you' (16:2, 4).

'*When that day comes,* you will not ask me for anything. . . . The Father will give you whatever you ask him for in my name. Until now you have not asked for anything in my name; ask and you will receive' (16:23, 24).

'*The time will come* when I will not use figures of speech, but will speak to you plainly about the Father. *When that day comes*, you will ask him in my name' (16:25, 26).

5. Life after death

If we have interpreted correctly all these sayings from chapters 13 to 16—and of course it is impossible to be certain—we are left with only one that appears to refer to the life beyond death:

'There are many rooms in my Father's house, and I am going to prepare a place for you. I would not tell you this if it were not so. And *after* I go and prepare a place for you, I *will come back* and take you to myself, so that you will be where I am' (14:2, 3).

Here and now

Thus we must conclude that at the time when Jesus is conveying the essential message of his Kingdom to his closest disciples, he is not preoccupied with the coming of that Kingdom at the end of time (as we might have expected), but he concentrates on the operation of his kingly rule here and now—in the crucifixion crisis, at the time of his Resurrection, in the era of the Holy Spirit.

Raymond Brown writes:

> Within Jesus' own message, there was a tension between realised and final eschatology. In his ministry the reign of God was making itself manifest among men; and yet, as heir of an apocalyptic tradition, Jesus also spoke of a final manifestation of divine power yet to come.

So we need not defer all our expectations to a distant happening. Much of what the implementation of God's reign means for us can be fulfilled in our present experience.

Praise God for all those things of which Jesus said, 'I am telling you the truth'! And praise God that so many of them are in the present tense, realisable in our experience now!

AND FINALLY . . .

Postscript

WE have already noted that chapter 21 may be a late addition to John's Gospel and that 20:30, 31 could be the original ending of the book:

> In his disciples' presence Jesus performed many other miracles which are not written down in this book. But these have been written in order that you may believe that Jesus is the Messiah, the Son of God, and that through your faith in him you may have life.

These verses point out that John's Gospel, as with the other Gospels, can only be a partial account of what happened. In a sense, every biography, however large, can only recount a fraction of its subject's thoughts, words and deeds. But these verses show that in this case the basis of selection has been very specific:

(a) to produce faith in Jesus as the Son of God (Messiah);
(b) to produce life through that faith, the kind of eternal life that renews us in time and revitalises us into eternity.

PPS

There is another conclusion in 21:24, 25:

> He is the disciple who spoke of these things, the one who also wrote them down; and we know that what he said is true. Now, there are many other things that Jesus did. If they were all written down one by one, I suppose that the whole world could not hold the books that would be written.

It looks as if verse 24 is a kind of authorisation from the leaders of the Church, at least in one place and at one time, similar to the imprimatur by which the Pope authorises Roman Catholic books. The verse identifies the writer as that same 'disciple whom Jesus loved' who has been referred to in 21:20, and who is usually accepted as John, the son of Zebedee.

Verse 25 makes the same point as the PS in 20:30. This is a partial biography designed as a gospel. The truth is limitless, especially if we go on to consider the work of the risen Christ through all the ages.

However, even in such detail as we have in John's Gospel, there is an abundant source of study and meditation. We have been looking at it from one point of view only, and the Gospel will repay much deeper study.

Lucas Grollenberg writes:

> It is certain that the writer [John] . . . has received a second gift, even more important than his direct or indirect knowledge of the facts . . . the gift which enabled him more deeply than any other disciple to penetrate the *meaning* of the person and work of Jesus and to express that in words and figures which will never become old-fashioned, for they are both Jewish and Greek, both biblical and universally human.

ALSO PUBLISHED BY
THE UNITED KINGDOM TERRITORY

My Father, our Father, a book of prayers for personal and congregational use, including prayers for special occasions, compiled by Lieut-Colonel Colin Fairclough.

This means war! by Major Chick Yuill, MA, who presents a Salvationist viewpoint of spiritual conflict against the forces of evil.

A beginner's guide to the Bible, a basic introduction to the contents of the Bible by Commissioner Leo Ward (R).

The Mercy Seat, by Captain Nigel Bovey who looks at the use of the mercy seat in the past and considers its continuing role in Salvation Army worship.

These books are obtainable from Salvationist Publishing and Supplies Ltd.